The Spiritual Guide

by
Michael Molinos

SeedSowers
Christian Books Publishing House
PO Box 3317
Jacksonville, FL 32206
www.seedsowers.com
800.228.2665

ACKNOWLEDGEMENT

The Spiritual Guide exists again today because of the unselfish donation of time by Mrs. JoAnne Chappell of Oklahoma City.

Copyright MCMLXXXII
by SeedSowers

Printed in the United States of America

SeedSowers
Christian Books Publishing House
PO Box 3317
Jacksonville, FL 32206
800.228.2665

ISBN 0-940232-08-1

CONTENTS

PREFACE

After having read this book it is really difficult to understand why the Roman Catholic church ever ordered *The Spiritual Guide* to be burned. With the exception of his oblique comment that it might *not* be necessary to take the sacraments or confession, there is really nothing that Michael Molinos said that was not first taught by other, greatly revered, Catholics. I think the problem lies not so much in what he said as in how successful he was in having said it and having aroused others to follow thereafter.

I was quite surprised to find that a large portion of this famous little book is given over, not to the deeper Christian walk, but to the cross and suffering! Frankly, I had not expected that. Before reading this book I would have guessed it to have a lot of practical help on how to know the Lord better. Certainly there is that; but it is also a spiritual primer on the cross. Molinos says it again and again: A great deal of suffering awaits us if we follow the Lord as we should.

The Spiritual Guide

The Introduction
by Michael Molinos

It is impossible to write a book that pleases everyone, and it is impossible to write a book that everyone understands. The question is, "What will be the book's relationship to you?" The subject covered herein is mysterious and not easily grasped. Such a book carries, therefore, a high vulnerability to criticism. But if you cannot understand the book, how can you censor it?

Now, Scripture tells us that the *natural* man does not understand the things which have spiritual significance. If you should criticize — or even condemn — though you do not understand it, you have joined yourself to the *world's* men of wisdom.

Understanding the deep things of the Lord does not come first from a good intellect, nor logic, nor reasoning; it comes through experience. The deep things of God are not invented things, *nor* are the teachings to be proven, but rather only to be received. This is why such matters are so fruitful in a believer's life. The deep things of the Lord do not come to the soul through your ear hearing nor your eye reading books, but by something the Holy Spirit puts in you abundantly. The Spirit's fruits He communicates to those who are humble in their mind and lowly in the use of their reasoning powers.

There are many wise people in the world today who have never read concerning matters in this book. There are others who are called spiritual men but who are not particularly fond of this subject. Both such men condemn the subject matter found in this book. One condemns out of ignorance and one condemns out of lack of experience.

But here is the essence of this matter. A believer who has not had the experience of what is discussed herein cannot pass judgement on the secret things of God. He may be scandalized when he hears of the wonders of divine love that are wrought deep inside a man, but this is because he simply does not know of these riches. But how shall any of us limit the goodness of God? After all, the Lord's arm is not shortened. He can do again in our day what He did so long ago. Remember your Lord calls neither the strong nor those of great merit. He calls the weak. He does this to show His great mercy.

What I speak of in this book is not something theoretical, but rather, practical — something within the realm of experience. Here, for all believers, is experience that surpasses the most refined and ingenious speculation. Spiritual matters really should be confined to those who are spiritual, though they never will be! If you happen to share these matters with someone who has stopped midway in his pursuit of Christ, then little, if any, benefit will come out of the sharing.

I have not written a particularly stylish book here. My only aim has been to teach naked truths, and that with all humility, sincerity and clearness. In this book I will not try to define or defend the Lord's ways.

It is the experience of many years that is recorded here, an experience which I have shared with many believers who have trusted in the very, very inefficient help which I have extended to them in their seeking toward an inward way. Because of what I have seen in these believers I am convinced that something is needed to remove obstacles, inclinations and allurements which hinder the Christian's progress toward the Lord's ends. What I have laid down here is what He has shown me in His infinite mercy, *not* that which I have taken out of books. My first goal is to simplify an understanding of the inward way.

May the Lord grant that this end be attained. I hope that some of you who read this, by His Divine majesty, are those called to plumb His depths, and that you will find profit in what I have written. If that occurs then I will be sure that my pains in writing this book were well employed. Such has been my only aim. If He chooses to accept and approve these pure desires then I shall be content to have my reward.

Michael Molinos
Rome, 1675

1

Two Kinds of Prayer

What is prayer? It is an ascent of the mind to God. He is above us all, and we cannot see Him, therefore we converse with Him. Such prayer as this is the simplest form of prayer. But this is a kind of prayer that is essentially only a mental discourse with God.

But when the believer fixes his attention on the face of his Lord without requiring consideration, reasoning, without need of proofs to be convinced of anything, *this* is a higher prayer.

There is a view of your Lord in which reason, meditation and thought do not play a large part. In the first kind of prayer, one *thinks* upon God; in the other, one *beholds* Him. The second is a purer practice.

Once a ship has arrived in the harbor, the voyage is over, is it not? In the same way, for us to truly lay hold of God there may be some means used to arrive there. But once those means have been established, and once the end has been laid hold of, you lay aside the means. That is, you lay down the method.

Sometimes a good place to begin *is* with rational prayer. Nonetheless, rational prayer is but a method to bring you to a deeper, more tranquil relationship with your Lord. When you have arrived at this second level of prayer you put an end to all rational discussion;

instead, you rest. A simple vision of God, seeing Him and loving Him (and very gently rejecting all the images which come into your mind): *This* is more meaningful prayer.

The mind is calm in the Divine presence. Everything within you is collected, *centered* and fixed wholly on Him.

It behooves you, you who would seek a deeper walk with your Lord, to soon lay aside clearly defined intelligibles. In short, lay aside *everything* and cast yourself into the bosom of a loving God. Eventually this Lord of yours will restore to you all you have dropped, while at the same time increasing you in strength and power. (I speak of a power to *love* Him more ardently.) In turn this love will maintain you in *all* circumstances that may come into your life. Be sure that the love which you pour out toward Him (which love He Himself will give you) is worth more than all the actions which you can ever perform. There is little you can do for God; there is so very little in this lifetime you will ever really come to understand of Him, I care not how wise you are, nor how much you study. But, oh! You can love Him a great deal.

When a believer begins to deal with the Lord on this second level he begins by a very simple method, that of drawing into a pure and deep center.

Your God is in this deep inward place, and it is in that place that loving attention, silence, and oblivion from everything else — *and* a surrender of the human will to the Divine will — may eventually be found. There, drawn into that place, the believer hears and talks with God alone. It is as though they were the only two things existing in all creation. Such "prayer" is a far cry from an intellectual discussion with God, or anything else which might be called prayer.

Rational conceptualization operates with toil, yet has

fruit. But this second kind of prayer I speak of operates without toil. There, in quiet and peace and delight, is found a far greater fruit.

Perhaps the first is necessary in order to have the second. The first is a seeking. The second is a finding. You might say the difference is as the difference between the preparation of food and the savoring of food.

Now I would say to you that there are two ways to walk in this deeper relationship with the Lord. The first you obtained through the exercise of a great deal of diligence, and — with divine grace assisting — by gathering together all your faculties and therein preparing yourself. The second way is not something that a man can do by his willpower; rather it is simply something which the believer eventually acquires!

2

The Desire to Lay Aside Outward Prayer

I would like to point out some matters which you might expect to encounter on a journey toward a deeper relationship with your Lord. Eventually you may come to a place where you find yourself unable to go on with an intelligent prayer life, *or,* at least, you will begin to *desire* to lay aside such prayer. This will not come to you by way of your natural inclinations nor because you are in a period of dryness, but rather it is provoked by the Lord Himself, deep within you. This inclination to lay aside a more outward prayer is the natural end of seeking, and hungering, for something deeper.

Another possibility you may notice is that the reading of books becomes a tedious matter. Perhaps this is because they do not deal with inward matters.

Another experience you might encounter is a growing knowledge of your own *self* nature, an abhorring of your sins, and an insight into the deeper nature of God, and His holiness.

What you are longing for is something that only the Lord can give you.

You will not fully know the inward life that I speak of until you know what it means for your own will to be conformed to that of the Divine will. If you, the believer, would have everything succeed, if you would have everything come to pass according to your own will, then you will never know the way of peace. Such a person will also lead a bitter and empty life, always restless and disturbed, never touching the way of peace. This deeper walk is in total conformity to the will of God.

Let me hasten to say that conformity is a sweet yoke, a yoke which brings us into those regions where lie inner peace and serenity.

What is the cause of a Christian's disquiet?

Rebellion of his own will is the chief offender. We do not submit to the sweet yoke of the Divine will and, as a result, we suffer many perturbing situations. Oh, Christian, if you submit your will to the Divine will, and to all His orderings, what tranquility you will know! What peace, what serenity.

These words shall be the main burden of this book. And may it please God to give me His Divine light, so that you and I may discover paths that lead us to this inward way.

3

An Inward, Invincible Fortress

Darkness, dryness, debilitating temptation — these are matters which God purges from the soul. First you should know that your spirit is the very center, the habitation, of the kingdom of God. (Your center *is* the Kingdom of God.) Your Lord reigns upon His throne, with rest, in that place. You will need to keep your heart in peace so that you may keep this inward temple of God a pure place.

Whatever the Lord sends into your life, there is no disturbance in that place.

For your good and for the profit of your spirit He will allow an envious enemy to trouble this city of rest, this throne of peace. Troubles will come to you in the form of temptations, tribulation, subtle suggestions. Anything and everything of God's creation may become involved in troubling you. There will be painful troubles and there will be grievous persecutions.

How are you to deal with such things? How can you be constant and cheered in your heart in the midst of all these tribulations? Enter into that inmost realm, for it is there you may overcome outward surroundings. Within you is a Divine fortress, and that Divine fortress defends, protects and fights for you.

Observe, please, a man who has as his house a great fortress; that man is not upset though his enemies pursue him and surround him. He need only retreat into the great citadel. *You* have a strong castle (deep within you) that will make you triumphant over *all* enemies — yes, those which are visible *and* those which are invisible. That castle dwells within you *now;* regardless of all snares and tribulations, *it is there!* Within it dwells the Divine comforter. Retreat there, for *there* all is quiet, peaceful, secure and calm.

How may you do this? The answer lies in that "deeper prayer" we spoke of earlier, and in that love which is wholly concentrated on Him alone.

When you see your peace assaulted, retreat to that region of peace; retreat to that fortress. If you find yourself fainthearted, retreat again. Here is an armor for overcoming the enemy and all other tribulations. Do not leave that place while the storm is on. Remain tranquil, secure and serene . . . *within.*

Lastly, don't be discouraged when you become fainthearted. If possible, return to that rich throne; collect all your thoughts; return to His face. Seek silence in the midst of the tumult, seek solitude in the masses, light in the midst of darkness; find forgetfulness in injury, victory in the midst of despondence, and courage in the midst of alarm, resistance in the midst of temptation, peace in the midst of war.

4

Expect Failure

You should know that every Christian who is called by the Lord to the inward way is, nonetheless, a Christian who is full of confusion and doubt, and one who has failed (and will fail) in this deeper level of prayer. In fact, you may get the impression that the Lord no longer helps you in prayer as He once did. You may feel you are losing a great deal of time and making no progress. Confusion and perplexity are bound to follow. Nonetheless, do not stop, and do not let anyone, even someone who is older in the faith, keep you from pursuing a deeper relationship with your Lord.

What is really happening in your life? Are you *really* experiencing failure? Not at all.

The Lord is calling you to walk by *faith* in His Divine presence. With a simple vision of your Lord and with intense love toward Him — like a little child would have toward its mother — cast yourself into the gentle bosom of your Lord. The spirit should become like a little child, and a *beggar,* in the presence of God.

Such a relationship to your Lord — especially in times of *perceived* failure — is *easy.* It is also *the most secure* relationship you can enter into with Him. The level of prayer you are seeking is a prayer free from a wandering imagination and from reasoning. Both of these are so distracting, and can get you involved in speculation and introspection . . . especially during periods of failure!

I would like you to remember that previous to giving Moses the Ten Commandments the Lord called Moses up on a mountain. There, for several days, the Lord showed him His great glory. I would draw a parallel to that incident. Often in the beginning of a Christian's quest God will introduce you into the school of loving knowledge and the school of the internal law. *Then* He will bring you into darkness and dryness. But why dryness? For exactly the same reason He introduced us to love! *To bring us near to Him.* Yes, dryness and failure draw us to Christ just as do encounters of love and touches of unseen realms. Your Lord brings you dryness because He knows so well that it is not by any means of your reasoning, nor your efforts, that you are going to be drawn near to Him. *Nothing* you will do can draw you to Him or Him to you. NO! Nothing! Your efforts *will not* bring you to understand His high and exalted ways.

How then shall you learn? By humble resignation to His will. *This* is where you will begin.

Noah is a perfect example of this. He was reckoned a fool by the world. But, later, the whole earth overflowed and he found himself in a raging sea without sails or oars. In all of those dark hours he walked by faith alone. Do not think he understood the mind of God. He did not.

As much as possible, then, be patient. Pay little attention to dryness or failures. *Do not give up your pursuit of a deeper kind of prayer.* Regardless of the amount of dryness and failure you encounter. Walk with a firm faith, dying to self and to all your natural efforts to know Him. Remember, He cannot err, nor does He intend anything toward you but that which is for your good.

Has it never occurred to you that when one is in the

process of dying, he must also suffer? How well is your time employed when you are dry, dumb, and resigned, yet sitting and waiting upon Him!

Here is something for you to consider: Divine blessing does not rest in your five senses.

Where, then, does the Divine blessing rest? The answer, again, is somewhere deep within you. Therefore come to Him, silent, believing, suffering, and with patience. With confidence press on. Rest in Him and be guided by His hand. This is better than all the goods in the world.

Look at the ox that grinds the meal. He seems to go nowhere and do nothing, yet he accomplishes a great work. Can that be called failure? It is not!

Remember this, the ox is receiving *nothing* of the corn but the master receives a great gift, and the master enjoys the produce of the ox.

If your pursuit of Christ is pure, that is sufficient reward.

A seed is laid in the ground. Then, it seems, the seed is lost. But afterward, when spring comes, that seed grows up and multiplies. God does the same thing with you.

Your Lord deprives you of comfort, and even of understanding. Furthermore you see no spiritual progress in your life. In a way, there is none! Yet, let enough time pass, and there *is* enrichment that has been added to you far beyond your hope.

Don't look down upon yourself if you cannot achieve what you have set out to in your pursuit of this matter of a deeper prayer. Hold your peace, and place yourself before your Lord. Persevere. Trust in His infinite grace, as though you were blindfolded. Do so without a great deal of thinking or reasoning. Place your life in His kind, paternal hands, resolving to do nothing except what is His Divine will and His Divine pleasure.

5

The Limitation of Outward Prayer

Throughout the ages it has been the common view of spiritual believers that the believer cannot attain to a deeper walk in relationship to his Lord by means of prayer that is mostly consideration, requests, meditation, reasoning and a great deal of objective discussion. At best such prayer is only of benefit *at the outset* of the spiritual quest.

Further, it has been observed, such surface and objective prayer is something that is learned very quickly.

But the relationship to Christ we are discussing here is *not* learned quickly.

If you continue on in typical — outward — prayer (prayer that is most common to those who pray), and if such practice continues year after year without a great deal of upward progression, then you are wasting a great deal of time. Why seek the Lord by means of straining the brain, in searching for some place to go to pray, in selecting points to discuss, and in straining to find a God without . . . when you have Him within you?

St. Augustine summed it up so beautifully:

> Lord, I went wandering like a stray sheep,
> seeking you with anxious reasoning

> weighted within me. I wearied myself much in looking for you without. Yet you had your habitation within me. If only I had desired you, and panted after you. I went around the streets and squares of the cities of this world and I found you not, because in vain I sought without for you who were within.

We simply shall not find our God without. Nor shall we find Him by means of reasoning and logic and surface information. Each of us has Him present within us. There seems to be a blindness in those believers who always seek God, cry for Him, long for Him, invoke His name, pray to Him daily, while never discovering that they themselves are a living Temple and His one *true* habitation.

Their own spirit is the seat and throne of a God who continually rests within them.

Who, then, but a fool would look for an instrument of God without when he knew that it was within his own door? Or who will ever be filled when he is hungry and yet refuses to ever taste? Yet, this is the life lived by many good men, always seeking, never enjoying. Their works are imperfect.

Nor should you think the spiritual way is difficult . . . nor is it only for those high minds.

Your Lord made it clear this was not true when He chose His apostles. They were ignorant and lowly. He spoke to the Father saying, "I thank you Father, that you have hid these things from the wise; You revealed them to babes." It is so clear that we are not going to attain to those deep things, nor those deep places within us, by reasoning or by surface prayer.

The Father takes care of the birds that are left when their own mothers turn away from them; do you think

He will abandon you? Consider those birds. They cannot speak and they have no reason, yet He cares for them and gives them the food that is necessary for them. They are not skilled in praying nice prayers, are they? Nor do they feel badly that they cannot say nice sounding prayers. Then why should you?

Actually, it is a good thing when you find yourself deprived of the pleasure of the senses and therefore find you must journey by the help of faith alone — yes, even to journey to the dark, deserted paths that lead to . . . where? You are not certain. Without such an experience it would be very difficult for you to reach certain places in your spiritual walk. A painful way of arriving, yes, but a *certain* one. Again I exhort you to be constant. Do not fall back, even though Divine discourse has left you and there is nothing for you to say in prayer.

6

Two Spiritual Experiences

In all your journey as a believer, you will have two categories of spiritual experiences. One is tender, delightful, and loving. The other can be quite obscure, dry, dark and desolate. God gives us this first one to gain us; He gives us the second to purify us.

First He deals with you as if you were only a child. *Then* He begins to deal with you as though you were a strong man. In the first there is a great deal of your Christian experience tied to that which you can sense outwardly. (You are attracted by these nice pleasant and outward experiences; in fact you can even become addicted to them.) But the other category of Christian experience calls for a believer to no longer mind the outward senses. Rather he must know warfare against his own passions, and attain to a will that is in complete agreement and concert with the Lord . . . this is the proper occupation of us all.

Dry spells are the instrument of God, for *your* good. Yes, it is true in such times, your five senses have been deprived and all *outward* progress of *outward* piety ends. Know this: In such times you are either going to leave off prayer, and perhaps even a large part of your Christian walk, *or* you will be driven to a comfort which has nothing to do with the outward senses.

There is always a veil that comes to us in relationship to times of dryness; it is a time when we do not know what He is doing. If we always knew what His working was (as He works *on* our outward man and works *in* our inward man) we would become very presumptuous. We would imagine we were doing quite well if we always knew what He was doing, would we not? We might even reckon that we had drawn very near to God. Such a conclusion would soon be our undoing.

A dependence upon outward circumstances, everything about your spiritual understanding depending on your outward senses — *all* of this must go by the way. How? By dryness!

The Lord uses these arid lands, these desert places.

The farmer sows in one season, and he reaps in another; God is quite like this. It is *in His time* that He gives you strength against temptation. (Often that strength comes at a time you least think it might.)

What are the fruits of a believer who persists in seeking the Lord in a deeper way in such times of dryness? Should you survive such periods and humbly persevere after Him, what might you expect to be the result of dry spells?

You will learn the gift of perseverance, which has many fruits and advantages. You will develop a weariness toward the things of this world little by little, and by slow degrees, the desires of your past life lose their strength; new ones toward your Lord arise.

You will also learn a reflection and concentration on things in which you formerly had virtually no interest.

When you are on the verge of committing some evil, you will sense some warning deep within you, a warning that will restrain you from the execution of that evil. Your attachment to that earthly pleasure will be cut, or you will flee from that situation or from that conversation, or whatever it is, that is drawing you away. You will be putting aside things in your life which never previously disturbed your conscience.

When you do fall into some fault, trusting it will be some light one, you will find a reproof within you which will afflict you greatly.

There will gradually grow in you a willingness, perhaps even a sense within you, that you are now willing to suffer and do the will of God.

There will also gradually grow up in you an inclination toward things holy (perhaps even an ease in dealing with the self nature, and with passions, and even with the enemy that waits in the way).

You will learn to know your self nature and despise it. Without this deep insight — even this revelation — all other attempts at "spirituality" are invalid. You will experience a great esteem for God, an esteem that is far above all other creatures. You will have a firm resolution not to allow yourself to abandon His presence, because leaving Him, abandoning Him, would be in itself the greater suffering and the greater loss.

You will have a sense of peace within you. A confidence in God's sovereignty and even a detachment from all other things.

All this can come about as a result of your persevering in prayer that is *dry* and *arid.* You will not feel these things when you are in prayer, but later, perhaps *much* later — *in His time* — when He and He alone considers it the appropriate time for you — these attributes will begin to appear.

All of the things that I have just mentioned, plus much more, are like new buds that arise from this little tree of spiritual prayer. Would you abandon such a small bush just because it seems to be dry, and because there is not much fruit on it, or because its buds seem so small and because it *appears* that there will *never* be any reaping? Dear one, be constant, persevere. Your soul will profit thereby.

7

Two Devotions

Just as there are two *prayers,* there are also two devotions. One devotion is real, and one is quite tied to the senses.

In devotion that is true there is not a particularly great *delight, nor* are there many *tears.* A devotion to the Lord which is based on the outward senses, the rational, the emotional (how you feel, what you think, your logical conclusions, outward circumstances, blessings, an onslaught of problems, confusion, doubt, poverty, poor health, wealth, good friends, an abundance of enemies, etc.), really should not be pursued at all. That devotion is actually an obstacle to progress and advancement in the internal way.

Some believers think that when their times with the Lord are pleasant, delightful and exciting, they are favored by God. Their next conclusion is that they possess Him and that they have a special walk with Him. They give their whole lives over to desiring this delightful relationship with Him.

But such ideas are wholly a delusion.

In a relationship to the Lord such as just described, everything is natural. Much of this may prove to be nothing more than a reflection (be it an emotional excitement or an intellectual stimulation) of your own nature.

This one thing is certain: Going no farther than this in your quest, concluding that *this* walk is the *right* walk and the most pleasing relationship to God, prevents the believer from acquiring a true relationship to the Lord. You must realize that thing which is deepest within you is *pure spirit.* It does not feel in the same way that the emotions feel. That which goes on inside the spirit is not outwardly perceptible as are those things which go on in the more outward portion of your being. Your spirit does not have to stand up and say that it *knows* what it loves, and *feels* what it loves; it does not *need* such things.

It is clear then if we are to be pressed into that which is more akin to the nature of the Lord (and not our own nature) we must pursue an inward walk. In doing this you will have to leave the guidance of your life to the Lord and expect Him to be your light in dry places, and even in dark places.

Remember you are not wasting your time "when nothing is happening." It has wisely been said, "Not to wait on God is the only great idleness."

It is idleness not to have leisure for God! Indeed, this is the business above all businesses. I would like to repeat for emphasis that to draw near to your Lord, to follow His internal inspiration, to receive His Divine influences in your inmost center, to reverence Him with your will, to cast away imaginations, concepts and ideas which occur during prayer — this is the way to true spiritual growth.

8

Two Kinds of Darkness

And now we come to another set of twos. There are two kinds of darkness, an unhappy darkness and a happy darkness.

The first darkness is that which arises from sin. It is a darkness that is filled with unhappiness and leads the Christian to eternal death. The second kind of darkness is darkness which the Lord allows within our inward part in order to establish and settle virtue. This is a happy darkness because it illuminates your inward spirit, strengthens it and gives it greater light.

Consequently, you ought *not* to be grieved and upset when your way is obscure and there is darkness around you. Nor are you to suppose you are lacking in the presence of God, that He has left you or does not love you. Further, the light you formerly possessed must not be seen as some great loss; nor the former relationship you had with the Lord — no matter how blessed it was and no matter that it has totally ceased to exist — as a great loss. It is not.

I would have you see these times of darkness as a happy darkness, a darkness in which you should persevere in your inward pursuit. It is a manifest sign that God, in His infinite mercy, is seeking to bring you into the inward path. How good will be the results, dear friend, if you will but simply embrace these times with peace and with resignation! Such times are for your spiritual good. These times of darkness *do not* slow you down in your journey toward Him! They may seem to, but in fact they hasten you toward the final point of your journey.

I would point out one particular matter here.

Perhaps you will come into darkness because you have had natural light removed from you. But remember that it may be in this darkness that you will first begin to find that supernatural *light,* within your *spirit* — a light which grows and increases in the midst of darkness! Often it is in times of dryness that wisdom and strong love are begotten.

(Of course, if, in times of darkness — or dryness — you turn away from practicing loving Him, or if you turn to worldly pursuits, these benefits will not be known to you.)

It is in *times of darkness* — not in times of great outward spiritual joy — that the self nature is dealt a mortal blow. Images, ideas, wanderings, and other hindrances — things which give you a distorted view of divinity — are consumed. Yes, it is by means such as those we have discussed here that the believer is led to the inward way.

Last of all, the Lord uses these dry times to purge your outward senses; this purging is necessary for your internal progress.

What then should be your view of dry times and dark times? They are to be *esteemed* and *embraced!* But, in times of darkness, what are you to do?

Believe.

Believe that you *are* before the Lord, *and* in His presence; continue to come to Him with sweetness and quiet attention. Don't try to discover things. Don't try to understand. Don't particularly try to seek a way out of darkness, and most of all do *not* stop coming before Him as you did in the most faithful time of your life and in those times when spiritual riches and blessings were at their highest!

Do not try to look for some emotion, or even a tender devotion, toward your Lord. Only express your desire to do His will and to be His pleasure. Otherwise you will simply go in circles throughout your life and take not even one step toward the inward goal. An emotional experience with Jesus Christ must not be your goal, for it is not His goal.

9

Loss of Spiritual Interest

Perhaps it will be your experience that soon after you have decided to die to a more external life and have moved toward His high mountain you will feel as though nothing is working in your favor! All the wonderful experiences you cherish will dry up. You will hardly be able to discuss spiritual things, or perhaps you will find you have gone so far as to not be able to conceive a good thought of God. Heaven will seem to have turned to brass and there will be little, if any, light. And when you turn back to concentration and thinking, even your thoughts will not be able to comfort you.

Be sure that, if this is the case in your life, your enemy will come to you with suggestion, unclean thoughts, impatience, pride, rage, cursing, confusion and much more. Perhaps you will even feel a distaste for the things of God. And you will feel you have lost some of the keenness of your spiritual understanding. Some will go so far as to feel there is no God, at least no God for them. You will wonder if you have even one good desire left in you.

Do not be afraid. These times and these things have a purging effect. You will grow in a sense of your own unworthiness, and in a realization of the need for your outward appetites to be dealt with. Only the Lord can cast the Jonah of your outward senses into the sea. Be sure that all of your strivings and thrashings are going to be worthless. Any external efforts of piety, or religion, or even of self denial, will *not* work. Rather, such things will aid in shining light upon you, a light that says, "You can do nothing. *All things* are in His hands and not in yours."

10

Circumstances

It is the nature of each of us to be rather base, proud, ambitious, full of a great deal of appetite, judgements, rationalizations, and opinions. If something does not come into our lives to humiliate us then surely all these things will undo us.

So, what does your Lord do? He allows your faith to be assaulted, even with suggestions of pride, gluttony, rage, perhaps blaspheming, cursing and yes, even despair. All of these serve to humble our natural pride, as a wholesome medicine within the midst of these assaults.

You know that Isaiah reminds us all that righteousness is just so many smelly rags — and that in spite of all our vanity, conceit, and self love.

Your Lord desires to purify your soul, and He can use a very rough file. Yes, He may even assault the purer and nobler things of your life! These assaults serve as a revelation to awaken the human soul . . . for the soul to *truly* discover, to truly know, just how miserable is its natural state.

And, if you seek spiritual counsel from someone during such times, it is possible that you may receive some help . . . but you would be very wise not to *expect* help.

Deep within you is a place of internal peace, and if you are to come through these periods and if you are not to lose that peace it is necessary for you to believe. You must believe in the fineness of Divine mercy . . . even when that mercy humbles, afflicts and tries you. How happy you will be if you will simply be quiet before the Lord! Even if these times are caused by the devil, you are nonetheless in the sovereign hand of God, and these things will turn out for your gain and your spiritual profit.

But perhaps you will protest and say, "My problems are not of that nature. It is not the Lord. It is not the devil. What is happening to me is from human hands, it is by my neighbor, by malice and injustice; it is being wrongfully treated."

It is true the Lord may not will someone else to sin against you, but He wills that the *results* of being sinned against turn out to His glory. He wills that you turn out improved in the area of patience.

When you are injured by another person whether he is a believer or not, there are two things involved. There is (1) the sin of him who did it, but also (2) a lesson for you. Perhaps more than a lesson. That sin of the other person may be against the Lord and may displease Him, but the destruction that it works in you is according to His will, and is for your good. Then what alternative do we have but to receive that will . . . to receive it as though it came directly from *His* hand? For it did.

For an illustration of this you need look no further than the life of your Lord. It was the wickedness and the sin of Pilate that caused the Lord's death, and yet we know His death was for our redemption.

It is so clear that the Lord makes use of someone else's fault for the good of your soul. How great is His Divine wisdom!

> Who can search out the depths of Your secrets, Lord! The wonderful ways and hidden paths to which you guide our soul, that it may be purged, transformed and changed into Your nature and content.

At the time of your conversion, your Lord came to dwell within you . . . in the spirit . . . the inmost part of your being.

Now for that celestial King to make even your *soul* His habitation, it is necessary that changes be wrought in your soul. The Lord purifies our soul as gold is purified in a terrible furnace of fire.

It is a certainty that the soul never really loves and believes more than at those times when it is afflicted. Whether you believe it or not (and whether you consent to it or not), those doubting and fears and tribulations that beset you . . . are nothing else but the refinements of His love.

If you need proof of this fact you need only look at the progress made in the soul when the conflagration is over.

First, there is a growing distrust of the self nature and a profound acknowledgment of the greatness and omnipotence of God; there is a greater confidence that the Lord will deliver you from all dangers. Furthermore, the mouth is more willing to confess with vigorous faith.

Therefore, dear one, look upon these difficult times as great happiness. The more you are beset the more you should rejoice, in peace. Do not be sad. Thank God for this favor which He is doing you. Simply despise what is happening to you. Nothing unnerves your enemy so much as when he sees himself despised in all that he is doing against one of the children of God.

Why? Because he realizes that all the things that he is doing, and suggesting, are of no avail.

Live your life as though you do not even see this one who is your enemy. Possess yourself in peace without anxiety. Do not ask to understand or even to question. Surely the most dangerous thing you can do is to rationally vie with the devil; after all, he is so capable in deceit.

Every child of the Lord must pass through a doleful valley and unjust onslaughts. You should be assured that with even the most saintly, the Lord continues dealing. Truly, they are those who pass through the greatest temptations. Why? That their crown will be greater, that the spirit of vain glory may be stopped, and that they may be kept firm in their relationship to Him.

11

Temptation

I would say that the greatest temptation is to be without temptations. The greatest onslaught is to be without any onslaught at all. Therefore be glad when you are assaulted. With resignation, peace and consistency . . . abide. There, in internal regions, walk and live.

You must walk the path of temptation. You will not walk down this road very far before you discover that the most internal parts of you (at least those which you can find) are scattered. Scattered and active, moving from one thing to another. There is a great deal of busyness down there!

How can you collect these many and divergent things that are happening within you?

Your Lord calls them together by *faith* and by *silence,* in the presence of God. Collect yourself in His presence with the one purpose and intent of loving Him. Come to Him as one who is giving himself to God. Behold Him in the most inward recess of your spirit that you can find. Do not employ imagination. Rest in love and come to Him in a general way of love and faith, coming for no specific claim, request or desire.

Deliver your life into His hands, to the end that He may dispose of you according to His good will and pleasure. Do not reflect on yourself nor even on some goal you might hope to attain, even if that goal is transformation! Move away from your emotions, but also move away from your rationality and logic . . . trusting God with all the care of your welfare. Pay no attention to the present affairs of your life.

As I have said, your faith should be pure, your love general; do not use your imagination or reasoning, do not concentrate on things of a distinct nature. Seek to unbusy your thoughts.

How do you collect all the scattered parts of your internal being?

You recall that Jacob wrestled with the Lord all night, until daybreak? *Then* it was that the Lord blessed him. You need such perseverance. Persevere against any and all difficulties which confront you in your seeking to collect your internal being. Do not desist until that bright sun of the Lord's internal light begins to appear within you. Be steadfast until the Lord gives your spirit His blessing.

I would assure you that after you have given yourself up to the Lord — to walk with Him and live in Him, *in an inward way,* all hell will conspire against you. Just one believer who has withdrawn into his inward parts makes a greater war against the enemy than a thousand whose walk is external. The enemy knows the infinite gain that comes to the believer who collects his internal nature.

Be careful about ambitions, even the ambition of being spiritual. You are here for God and not for yourself. The Lord esteems more important the problems you have in trying to still yourself inwardly than in all your ambition to be great in the Kingdom of God.

You are going to try to resist your wandering thoughts, but this will probably leave you more anxious than if you don't resist them! It is better, in your weakness, to peacefully yield up to God all these troubles of a wandering mind. Then return to Him as long as your wandering thoughts allow. You may sense no light; you may sense nothing spiritual happening to you. Do not be disturbed. Collect yourself once more. And then resign yourself to steadfastness.

> Whether my thoughts choose to wander from Him, or if they forever wander from Him, as oft as I become aware that I have wandered, just so often will I yield myself back up to Him with no thought of frustration because my mind wandered.

Do you believe when you have come from prayer that is dry, that it was because of poor preparation and that the time you spent before Him has done you no good? If you do, then your belief is fallacious. Genuine prayer does not consist in enjoying the Lord, nor enjoying His light. *Nor is it in having gained knowledge of spiritual things.*

(You can learn about spiritual things from speculative understanding. You can also have total mastery of all such things and still have nothing of the Lord's virtue nor of His transforming work.)

The consistency of true prayer is in *faith,* and in *waiting* on Him. First you *believe* that you are in His presence. You *believe* that you are turning to Him with your heart. And you wait there before Him, tranquilly. These are the only preparations that you need. The *final* results contain a great deal of fruit.

You may expect the enemy to come to you, to disquiet you and cause you trouble, for that is his nature. You will find that the nature of those things you have always enjoyed — pleasures your outward senses have derived from spiritual things — (including areas in which you are gifted) . . . all these will become weak.

You might even expect weariness. All exercise can become difficult. Whether you have these, or other problems . . . *persevere!*

You can expect to suffer through problems of a multitude of thoughts, problems of the imagination, provocation of your natural desires, and problems of an inward life that is very dry. All of these temptations must yield to the spirit.

Though these situations are all referred to as *dryness,* truthfully they are very profitable. That is, they are profitable if you embrace them and receive them with patience.

And if it seems to you that you have done nothing in the time that you have set aside for the Lord, do not be deceived. A good heart — a firmness in prayer — is something that is very pleasing to your Lord.

When we come to the Lord in this way we labor *without* personal interest. We labor merely for the glory of God. Surely it may seem that we wait in vain, yet this is not so. We are as the young men who work in the field with their father. At the end of the day, unlike the hired labor, we receive no pay.

But at the end of the *year,* we enjoy *all* things.

12

Self Seeking, In the Seeking of God

God loves not the believer who does the most, nor who feels the most, nor who thinks the most cleverly and best, nor even that one who shows the greatest love, but He loves him who suffers the most.

I am aware that in telling you that a deeper prayer is a prayer that does not depend on outward senses nor on those things which are pleasing to our natural man, that we are speaking of something that requires the martyrdom of some parts of us. But, please remember, we are also speaking of something that pleases the Lord.

When there is no emotional experience nor intellectual insight into His way, the enemy may suggest to you that God has not spoken. But your Lord is not impressed with a multitude of words. He is impressed with the purity of the intent of your heart. He wishes to see the inward part of you humbled, quiet, and totally surrendered to Him and to His will, whatever it may be. You may not find emotions to produce such a relationship, but you will find a door by which you will enter into your nothingness and His all.

There are those people who *have* begun a practice of collecting their inmost being but turned away from it almost immediately because they did not find any *pleasure* in it! There was no sense of God, there was no power, there was no sense of being pleased with their own thought, or being impressed with the way they formed their words and sentences to God. Actually all of these approaches to God *are nothing but a hunt for sensible pleasures.* This, to God, is but self love and seeking after self. It is really not a seeking after God at all.

It is *necessary* that you suffer a little pain and a little dryness. Without thinking about how much time you have lost or what other losses you have sustained, come to the Lord with reverence, paying no attention to dryness and sterility. You will find eternal reward.

The more your outward man delights in some sort of pleasure in prayer, the less delight there is in the Lord. But the less you care for the outward thrills of spiritual things . . . ah, *here* is something which delights the Lord.

13

Tranquility

Remember that it is *tranquility* which you will use to repel wandering thoughts and temptations.

When you go to prayer, deliver your entire being into the hands of God, and do so with perfect resignation and with an act of faith; believe that you stand in His presence and remain there quietly. And, as I have said, with tranquility.

(Do you fret over a wandering mind? Is this evidence of a life totally given over into His hands, accepting all things from His hands?)

Let me illustrate. If you have given a precious jewel to a dear friend, once it has been given to him, it is not necessary for you to repeat, "I give you this jewel, I give you this jewel." All that needs to be done is to let him keep it! Do not take it from him! Surely, if you do not take it back from him, it is certain that you have given it to him.

Do not labor in constantly reminding the Lord of your commitment and resignation to Him. You have given Him the jewel; do not take it back.

And how would you take it back?

Only by committing some noteworthy fault against His Divine will.

****

The mere business of getting ready to go before the Lord is great preparation. It awakens your lively sense toward what it is you are doing.

Hold always before you this simple fact, that your response in God abides in peace.

You are involved in learning love; therefore you must learn to retreat from the multiplication of fervent acts, outward duties, and services . . . for all of these are primarily accomplished by the outward senses. Nor am I suggesting you lay aside these activities in order to pick up such things as delight, tenderness, and sweet sentiments. These may not be outward activities and they may even have some small spiritual part to them; nonetheless they are mostly a blend of the things of the natural. Your soul is to love your Lord *without any kind of impediment,* not even the impediment of spiritual blessing.

Neither desire to act nor be thinking of many things, but rather plunge yourself into faith.

I would like to refer to Madame de Chantal. Here is a letter she wrote to one of the Lord's servants:

> I felt myself dedicated to Him, absorbed and reposed in Him. This simple view of God continued in me by grace. But then I gave way to fear, thinking myself unworthy, unprofitable in this state. A desire to perform good deeds and serve the Lord came to me — but if I am to follow my internal impulse, then I must lay aside all else. When I consider strengthening my being with reasoning, dedications and acts of service, I cannot do so except by exertion. But He would have all things done by Divine activity. The more I retain in my in-

most parts an attitude of quiet tranquility, the better all else succeeds. I should never look at myself, but walk with eyes shut, leaning on my beloved, without striving to see the way, nor to know the way that He is guiding me; neither fix my thoughts on anything nor beg favors of Him, but remain truly effaced and quiescent in Him.

14

A Commitment Established

Many have said this to me: "I've come to the Lord with perfect resignation toward all things. I have given myself to His presence by an act of faith. Yet I have not acquired any improvement. The reason is, my thoughts are so distracted that I cannot fix them upon God."

Don't be upset or discouraged; you have lost neither time nor merit. Do not lay aside your quest. When you come before the Lord, it is not necessary that you think upon the Lord. It is only necessary that you continue in your progress.

Your imagination may ramble over an infinite number of thoughts, yet, I assure you, the Lord has not left. Continue your perseverance in prayer. Remember that He prays within you, and He prays in spirit and in truth. The distraction of the mind — which is not intended — does not rob the prayer of its fruit.

But, I am asked, "Am I not at least to remember that I am in the presence of God? Am I not to say to Him, 'Lord, You abide within me and I give myself wholly to Thee'? Surely I should at least pray this."

No, there is no necessity for it. You have a desire to pray and to that end you went before Him. Faith and intention are always enough. These always continue. The simpler your remembrance is — without words or thoughts — the better foundation you lay for an undistorted relationship with the Lord who abides in you.

I am also asked, "Would it not be proper to say, 'Lord, I believe Your majesty is here'?" This is the same as the above. With the eyes of faith the spirit within you sees God, believes in Him and stands in His presence. The inmost portion of your being has no need to say, "My God, Thou art here." Believe.

Your spirit always believes.

Your spirit *knows* He is there.

Go, then, to that place where belief and knowing are always present.

And how do you go there? By faith alone.

When the time to be before the Lord has come, know that your friend *faith,* and your friend *intention,* will guide and conduct you to God. You arrive there by means of an act of faith and by a perfect resignation on your part as you wait in His presence.

If you do not retract your faith and your intention, then you walk in faith and resignation, and therefore you walk in prayer.

A mountain does not say, "I am a mountain." Nor does a woman walk around saying, "I am married, I am a wife, I am a wife." Do you walk around saying, "I am a Christian, I am a Christian"? If you never think about it, still you are a Christian. The woman is still a wife and the mountain still a mountain.

The Christian is obligated to do no more than this: to believe more with his heart than he does with his mouth. The wife gives a demonstration of her fidelity to her husband by the very life she lives. Once the Christian has resolved to believe that the Lord dwells within him, and that he will henceforth seek the Lord, and do nothing but what he does through God . . . once that has been done, the Christian should rest . . . *satisfied in the faith* which is in his spirit.

Repetition of this matter is not necessary.

15

Your Occupations and Your Call

Your daily occupations are not contrary to your Lord's will. Your occupation is not against the resignation to His will which you presented to Him. You see, resignation encompasses all the activities of your daily life. Whether it be study, reading, preaching, earning your living, doing business, or the like . . . you are resigned to whatever it is that comes into your life each day, each hour, each moment. Whatever happens in your life is, in itself, *His will.* You have not left that resignation of will *nor* have you left His presence.

If you are drawn away from Him - if you are drawn away from prayer — revert to God, return to His presence — then renew an act of faith and renew an acquiescence to His will.

And what of dryness? Dryness is good and holy, and *cannot* take you from the Divine presence. *Do not call dryness a distraction!*

When a man sets out on a journey to a great city, every step he takes is voluntary; he does not need to say, "I wish to go to the great city, I wish to go to the great city." That first step is an indication of his intention. He journeys without saying it, but he cannot journey without intending it.

I realize it is true that all Christians have faith, and those who practice an objective and outward prayer also fit this illustration. But the faith of those who journey by the inward way is very different. Theirs is a living faith. It is without images. It is effectual and enlightened . . . to the extent, that is, that the Holy Spirit enlightens the spirit within us. And a man's spirit is stronger when his mind has been collected toward his God.

In proportion to that recollection there is an inner illumination.

16

Two Kinds of Spiritual Men

There are two kinds of spiritual men. And they are contrary to one another.

Some tell us that the mysteries and the sufferings of Christ are always to be meditated upon. Others, at the other extreme, tell us that the only true prayer is an internal thing, offered up in quiet and silence, a *centering* upon the exaltation and supreme Diety of God.

Let us look at our Lord. He has said, "I AM the Way, the Truth, and the LIFE." Before anyone can come into the presence of Divinity, he must be washed with the precious blood of the Redeemer . . . hence we are certain we should *not* lay aside the redemption of our Lord. But neither should we tell a believer who has learned something of living within his spirit that he should always be reasoning, meditating and considering the suffering and death of our Lord.

As long as an outward prayer nourishes and benefits, a believer should follow outward prayer. It is only when a longing for something more is sensed in the heart that the pilgrimage into the inward way should be considered. It is up to the Lord alone to take us from one to the other. St. Paul, in writing to the Colossians, exhorted them as well as us that whatever we do, whether it is in word or deed, we should do it in the name and for the sake of Jesus Christ. May God grant that you and I, in Him and through Him alone, may arrive at that state which most pleases him.

17

Three Kinds of Silence

There are three kinds of silence: a silence of words, a silence of desires, and a silence of thoughts.

The first is perfect. The second is even more perfect and the third is the most perfect.

In the first, the silence of words, there is virtue that is acquired. In the second, the silence of desires, quietness is obtained; and in the third, the silence of thoughts . . . *this* is the goal: the internal recollection of all of your senses. To lay hold of the silence of thought is to arrive and abide at the center of your being, where Christ dwells.

By not speaking, desiring, nor reasoning, we reach the central place of the inward walk — that place where God speaks to our inward man. It is there that God communicates Himself to our spirit; and there, in the inmost depths of our being, He teaches us Himself. He guides us to this place where He alone speaks His most secret and hidden heart. You must enter into this through all silence if you would hear the Divine Voice within you.

Forsaking the world will not accomplish this. Nor renouncing your desires. No, not even if you should renounce all things created!

What then?

Rest is found only in this threefold silence . . . only before an open door, where God may communicate Himself to you. It is in that place that He transforms you into Himself.

The transformation of your soul consists not in speaking to God nor in thinking on God, but in *loving Him greatly*. And how is this love acquired? By means of perfect resignation, and by this threefold silence. The love of God has but few words.

> My little children, let us not love in word, neither with the tongue, but in deed and in truth.

Perfect love does not consist of such things as loving acts, not in tender offerings of words, nor even in internal acts where you tell the Lord that you have a great love for Him. In all of these you may yet be seeking yourself and exalting your self nature rather than engaging in knowing God.

Love is not found in fair discourse.

Here is a man given to a great deal of thinking and rationalizing. If he wishes to know something about you then you will have to express yourself in words. But such is not God. He searches the heart. Nor does He need to hear you affirm to Him your love nor explain yourself to Him.

Neither is He satisfied with a love that is presented to Him by your tongue.

For instance, you may tell the Lord, with all the zeal and fervor of your being, that you love Him . . . tenderly and perfectly . . . yet when you are slightly injured, you offer some bitter word rather than resigning yourself and going to the cross for the sake of your love for Him.

Such an act is proof that your love was tongue and not deed.

Seek to resign yourself, therefore, to all things around you. Do so with this threefold silence. In so doing you will have truly told Him that you love Him. Not in words at all, but in that more perfect love. It is a quiet and effectual love, this.

Peter told the Lord that he was ready to lay down his life for Him, and yet with the words of a young girl his zeal ended. On the other hand Mary Magdalene did not say one word to him, and the Lord looked at her and said, "She loves much." It is *internally,* then that the most perfect virtues of faith, hope, and love are practiced. There is no need to be telling God that you love Him, that you hope in Him and believe in Him. The telling of it is nothing. The Lord knows better than you do what is going on in your heart.

Oh, our Lord, how well did You know how to penetrate into the inmost parts, and to distinguish between the outer and the inward man!

18

Obedience

You will never attain to the mountain of internal peace if you govern yourself according to your own will. This self nature of your soul must be conquered. Your directions, your judgement, your disposition to rebel must be subjected and reduced to ashes. How? In the fire of obedience, for it is there that you will find out if you are truly a follower of Divine love or self love. There must come a holocaust of your own values and judgements and will.

One of God's servants once said:

> It would be better that you gather dung by obedience than be caught up into the third heaven by your own will.

Now, everyone enjoys the idea of honoring and obeying *superiors.* But it is also necessary, if you are to follow the inward way, to obey and honor your *inferiors* as well.

What is true obedience? Obedience, to be perfect, must be voluntary; it must be pure and cheerful. But most of all it must be *internal.* I would add that it must also be blind and persevering.

Volunteer to obey without fear; and *never* engage in obedience if there is fear. Obedience that is *pure* has no personal interest or thought of gain for oneself. Pure obedience is solely for the gain of God. Obedience is ready at any time, with no excuse and no delay. It is *cheerful,* without inward resentment, and *internal,* because it must not be external.

Obedience must proceed from the heart, *blind* because it must put aside a judgemental nature and private judgement.

When you fall into a fault, do not be unduly troubled, and certainly do not afflict yourself for falling. Faults are but the results of our frail nature and of the Fall. Why do you marvel? Humble yourself, knowing that you have seen your own misery. Thank God that He has preserved you from endless sin into which you might have fallen by following your own inclinations and appetite.

What can be expected from this slippery ground (our own nature) but briars and thistles and thorns? It is a miracle of Divine grace that we do not fall every moment into innumerable faults. Your enemy will make you believe, at the time you fall into some fault, that you are not well grounded in the ways of God, that you walk in error, that you are not truly repentant, and that therefore, you are without God.

If you happen to *repeat* the fault, then your enemy escalates his accusations against you even more. He will tell you that your pursuits toward God are in vain and that they are availing nothing, that your time spent before the Lord is fruitless. Oh Christian, open your eyes and do not allow yourself to be carried away by the deceitful and gilded tricks of the enemy. He is seeking your ruin through despair and lies and suggestions. Check these reasonings. Relinquish these considerations. Shut the gates against these diabolical accusations. Acknowledge the misery of your natural state and trust in the mercy of God. And if tomorrow you fall again, then trust again in the goodness of your God, who is so ready to forget your faults and receive you into His arms as a child.

If you are going to follow the Lord in a way that is high (and an inward way) then you must use the weapon of confidence — confidence in Divine goodness. You must use the weapon night and day and *use it always when you fall.* A loving and humble conversation with Divine mercy is something you must exercise in the midst of all your faults and imperfections.

What God does to deliver us He sometimes does in 40 years, and sometimes in an instant; this is a singular mystery. The Lord does not let us know which He will do; this mystery, therefore, demands that we live in humility. Whether it be in 40 years or an instant, it is the work of His powerful hand that frees us from sins.

It is a rather dangerous thing to be perfect. There is vice in being without frailty; there is vice in virtue.

> Because we make a wound of our medicine He makes a medicine of our wound, so that we who are injured by virtue may be cured by vice.

The Lord, by means of our small failures, lets us know that it is His majesty which frees us from great faults. These are the ways He keeps us humble and vigilant.

And if you fall a thousand times you just make use of this remedy: a loving confidence in Divine mercy. These are the weapons with which you must fight and conquer cowardice and vain reasoning.

19

Internal and External Spirituality

There are two kinds of spiritual people, those who are internally spiritual and those who are externally spiritual. Those who are spiritual externally seek God by reasoning, by the things they imagine, by long periods of consideration in which they go down many avenues of thought.

These people endure pain to obtain virtue. They delight in talking about God. They delight in being very fervent in love, and even in being skilled in prayer. They are seeking to obtain greatness by *doing* things. They believe that God abides close to them only by their doing the above-mentioned things.

What is this?

This is the way of beginners! Experience has shown that many believers, even after 50 years of this external exercise, are void of God. They are also full of themselves, having nothing of the true spiritual man except the name.

But there is another spiritual man, the one who has passed beyond the beginning and walks toward the inner way. Such believers withdraw into the inward parts of their spirits and there relinquish everything about themselves into the hands of God. They have forgotten and despoiled themselves of everything. And not only *things,* but *themselves!*

With an uplifted face and an uplifted soul, they come into the presence of their Lord. They come by faith. They come there without imagining what God is like nor forming some picture of Him. They come to Him with assurance — assurance that is found in tranquility and in inward rest. They come, having collected their entire consciousness and centered all their being in one place — on Him.

You can be sure that such people have also passed through a great deal of tribulation, and all of that tribulation came to them because it was ordained by His hand.

In everything they have denied themselves.

True, they are still subject to temptation, but out of temptation and tribulation come infinite gain. It is God who fights the battle from within them.

There is no news that causes them to overabundantly rejoice nor is there any news that fills them with sadness.

Tribulation cannot unnerve them; yet they have a holy fear before the Lord, resting only in their communion of heart with Him.

Those who seek the Lord *externally* have to always *do* something . . . outward mortification, efforts at destroying certain weaknesses, battles with desires, or the acquiring of spiritual knowledge, scriptural information, etc. But whatever external efforts we employ to know God, these will produce little or nothing. We cannot do anything of ourselves. That is, nothing *except* things that are miserable.

But what of the *inward* way? The inward way is a centering of the whole being in a loving manner in the Divine presence. There, *the Lord* operates! It is by Him that virtue is established; it is by Him that desires are eradicated; it is by Him imperfections are destroyed.

The believer has entered into the chambers of his spirit and there he lives in spirit without those great efforts of struggling. He finds himself free. Freed from so many things which the external way simply can never release him from.

It is by an illuminating light that a follower of the Lord understands his own miseries, weaknesses, and imperfections. And though he abhors what he really is, nonetheless he is before the Lord in loving fear. There is contempt and mistrust of self, but there is hope in God.

The more we come humbly before the Lord with true contempt of what it is we are, the more pleasing we are to God. The spiritual man comes to stand in His presence with wonder and veneration of the One before whom he stands.

And when he comes before the Lord he does not bring into the Divine presence any mention or thought of any good works that he has done or any suffering that he is going through. Rather, it is his continual exercise to withdraw deep within, into God. There, before his Lord, at the center of *His* habitation, the spiritual man knows this inward withdrawal is far more important than speaking of God or even speaking *to* God. He withdraws into the inner and secret center of the spirit, there to *know* his Lord and to receive His Divine influence . . . with fear and with loving reverence.

But you must know that there are very few believers who arrive at such a happy state. Why? Because few of us are willing to embrace contempt, to suffer the purification of transformation of our inward parts, and to keep humbly before Him without being proud of seeking Him, or proud of humility, or proud of our (supposed) attainment.

Perhaps many — even most — believers really desire to seek after God and to walk with God. Yet, most get stuck at the entrance. And why? Because few of us are willing to die, and it is in this *disposition* (dying) that so sovereign a gift is found.

****

Here is the way to cease deceiving yourself: recognize the difference between the outer and the inner way. The difference is the presence of God. His presence, which you practice by faith, is entered by your collecting your center, and then waiting before the Lord. This is how you learn the difference between the outer man and the inner man.

If you imagine that the life that is being described is a life full of goodness and full of the ability to suffer evil, then you are deceived.

You should have no desire for what will come out of your having an inward walk with God.

Your desire must be to end *your* life for *His* sake. The way of your Lord was not sweetness and softness! And He never invited you, or anyone, into such a thing.

> If any man come after Me, let him *deny* himself and take up his *cross* and *follow* Me.

The believer who would be united with Christ must follow Him in the way of suffering.

****

If you do begin to taste the sweetness of Divine love it will only be a matter of a very short time before the enemy comes to you and kindles in your heart a desire to go to the desert and there live before God in solitude. The enemy, mind you, reasons with you, saying you will be able to live before Him without hindrance and there — as a result — you will continually *delight* in prayer. This reflects a very immature understanding of the Lord's ways. And it shows that you wish to have the

Lord for the delights and thrills which result from living in His presence.

There are many Christians abroad who have received from the Lord magnificent revelations, great visions and a great grasp of high mental truths. Yet for all of this they do *not* deeply understand those hidden secrets which come to those who have gone through great *temptations* and *trials.*

What great fortune it is for your soul when it is subdued!

What an honor it is to be despised. What elevation to be beaten down. What comfort to be afflicted. What high knowledge to seem as ignorant. What happiness of all happinesses it is to be crucified with Christ. *This* is the lot which the Apostle Paul gloried in:

> Forbid it for me to glory save in the cross
> of our Lord Jesus Christ.

Let other believers glory in the riches, dignity, delights, and honors that some circles afford the successful believer. But to us there is no higher honor than to be denied, to be despised and to be crucified with Christ.

It is a great grief that, among believers, only a few despise spiritual pleasure! So few.

There are not many who are willing to be denied for Christ and embrace His cross with love.

Many *do* launch out into the inward way. But, be sure, only a few come to the end of its path. This is because there are few who embrace the cross — that is, few who embrace it with patience, constancy, peace, and resignation.

To always follow those things which are contrary to the will of your own nature is something few Christians can do.

Furthermore, many teach these things, but very few practice them.

Many believers begin this walk and persevere very well just as long as there is still sweetness and delight in their fervor. But *as soon* as the delight of His presence *disappears* these believers are overtaken by trouble, dryness, and temptation. Some, perhaps most, turn back.

Do you not understand that trouble, that dryness, that temptation are necessary things to a person to go through along the high road to the mountain of God's perfect will?

Those eager Christians who falter and turn back give a clear sign that they sought the high things of God and the deep things of God for *themselves* and *not* for God.

If you are one who has been given light concerning an inward walk, then be constant in dryness, constant in temptation, and constant in tribulation . . . and do not turn back.

Do not be guided by self-love.

This monster must be vanquished if we are to reach the high summit of the mountain in peace.

Remember, too, that this monster is everywhere present in your relationship to those who are your kin . . . especially if you have allowed yourself to be *unduly* addicted to your family's pleasure or displeasure.

Sometimes the stumbling of self-love is found in pleasing the religious guide who is over you, sometimes in vain glories and pleasant little honors. There is also the cleaving to spiritual pleasures, laying hold of the gifts of God and then *holding on* to them! Concealed under all of these is the desire for good treatment and personal comfort. And all of them smack of self-love. They must all come down. That is, they must come down if you are to arrive at that place where peace is enthroned.

20

Cleansing the Soul

There are two ways for the soul to be cleansed. The first is through affliction, anguish, distress, and inward torment. The second is through the fire of a burning love, a love impatient and hungry.

It is true that sometimes the Lord uses both of these ways to deal with our souls. *All* revelation and insight into God, all true experiential knowledge of God, *arises from suffering,* which is the truest proof of love.

Oh, how I hope and wish for you that you can understand the great good that comes from tribulation. Tribulation cleanses the soul. The cleansing of the soul through tribulation is what produces patience.

Within tribulation can come inflamed prayer.

In the midst of tribulation we can exercise the most sublime acts of love and charity. To rejoice in the midst of tribulation brings us near to God. It is tribulation which annihilates and refines. It is that which takes the earthen and transforms it to the heavenly. Out of the human it brings forth the divine . . . transforming one and bringing it to the other, uniting them with the Lord.

Oh Christian, if you would know how to be *constant* in the fire of tribulation and *quiet* in the fire of tribulation, to be washed with the waters of affliction, then you would discover just how soon divine goodness would make its throne in your soul. There, in that good habitation, God would be able to refresh and solace Himself.

How much is gained by knowing the internal and external cross! And when tribulation does befall you, keep constant . . . for things are not as they seem to you during tribulation.

Be not deceived in the midst of tribulation . . . there is *no time* in your life when you are nearer to God than in the time when He has deserted you! The sun may be hidden behind the clouds, yet the sun has not changed its place, nor has one bit of its brightness been lost. The Lord allows a painful desertion of His presence from within you to purge and to polish you, to cleanse you and to despoil *the self!* Your Lord does this so that you might have a clear-cut opportunity to give your whole being up to Him without any notice of personal gain . . . but rather only to be His delight.

Although you may be groaning and lamenting and weeping, yet in the most secret and hidden places of your inmost being He is joyful and glad.

21

Divine Love

There is a fire of Divine love.

It is this love which burns the believer and can even cause the believer to suffer. How? Sometimes the absence of the Beloved greatly affects the believer.

Sometimes the believer hears the inward voice of the Beloved calling. It is as a gentle whisper and proceeds from out of the believer's inmost depths . . . where the Lord, the Lover, abides. It is this whisper which possesses the believer almost to the point of undoing. The believer realizes how near is his Lord and yet he also realizes how much of the soul has not yet been possessed by Him.

This intoxicates the believer and puts an insatiable longing within him to be changed into the likeness of his Lord. Therefore, it can be said of love: Divine love is as strong as death, for it kills just as surely as death kills.

****

You will know that you are far from perfection if you do not find God in everything.

Know that pure, perfect love consists of these elements: the cross and denial of yourself. Both of these elements are totally voluntary. These, plus accepting — with resignation — all things which come into your life . . . in humility . . . then relating all these things to your spirit . . . then adding a mean opinion of your self-nature —these are the elements you must have in your life.

In seasons of desolation or in seasons of temptation, I would urge you to always learn to withdraw into the inmost chamber of your spirit. There, do nothing but behold God. It is in the depth of your spirit that is the place of true happiness. It is *there* that the Lord will show you wondrous things.

When we are therein engulfed and lose ourselves in the immeasurable sea of His infinite goodness and abide in it, steadfast and immovable, we have fulfilled our lot. There is found the reason for our existence.

It is to the believer who has, with humility and resignation, reached this deep place of seeking only to fulfill God's will, that the Divine and loving Spirit teaches all things with a sweet and life-giving function.

High and sovereign is the gift of that one who can suffer the cross both internally and externally with contentment and resignation.

What does it mean to be perfectly resigned? It means that the believer resolves to abide with God alone, esteeming with equal contempt those things called *gifts* and those things called *light* and *darkness*. The believer lives only in God and for Him.

Happy is the man who has no other thought but to die to his self-nature. Therein is a victory over the enemy. Yes, but there is also victory over self. In that victory you will find a pure and unadulterated love, and a perfect peace toward your Lord. The believer who leaves *all* to find the Lord begins to possess all for eternity.

There is a great difference which lies between this thing of *doing* and this thing of suffering and dying.

Doing is delightful. It belongs to beginners in Christ. Suffering belongs to those seeking. Dying — dying to the self — belongs to those who are being completed in Christ.

****

Enjoyment and inner peace are the fruits of the Divine Spirit. No man lays hold of these two elements unless he finds them in the depths of his spirit, and unless he resigns all things that come into his life as being from the hand of God.

Keep silent and let your conversation be something that is internal. Deny and put to death your self-nature by not judging ill of anyone at any time. Your suspicion of your neighbor troubles the purity of your heart; suspicion and criticism disquiet the heart; they bring the believer out of the realm of the spirit and take away his rest.

You will never be fully resigned to the will of God if you are troubled by human opinion of you, or if you make for yourself a little idol of what people say.

****

One of the healthiest things you can do in order to learn to walk in the inward way (and to lose yourself) is to look upon reason and "sound logic" as something that is created. The most *reasonable* conduct you can perform is to discard a great deal of your reasoning. Believe God. Believe the He permits grievances to fall into your life, for it is true. He *does* allow grievances into every life lived on earth. He does this so that we may be humbled, and so that certain aspects of our nature may be annihilated. He does these things so that we may live in complete resignation to his will. Your Lord pays *more* attention to that believer who lives in an internal resignation than He does to all those who work miracles . . . even to the raising of the dead.

****

It is a saying worthy of all truth that a person who despises his own self-nature cannot be hurt or injured by someone else. Let nothing disturb you. Let nothing affront you. All things will come to an end. God only is unchangeable. Patience obtains all things. He who has God has everything. He who has not laid hold of God has nothing. If you are impatient toward another and you lay the fault on your companion, then you never realize that *you* are *intolerable!*

When the rancor is over, it is your cunning ability to rationalize which proves you to be virtuous! Virtue so attained is a poor virtue indeed.

And why not? After all, you give precepts. You relate spiritual sayings. You relate all things to Scripture. Yet you do this without your faults ever changing.

Oh yes, you are willing to say things about yourself, to disclose your faults before others, and many other such impressive things; but *within* you, you are *justifying* yourself far more than you are seeing your faults! By such means the monster within you returns again and again to esteem himself.

Or perhaps you say: "This matter is not because of some fault in me, but because of my zeal for justice"! This only shows that there is something within you that still believes that you are virtuous, courageous, constant, and that you would give your life up to death for the sole sake of Divine love. Yet you can hardly hear a bitter word against you without being troubled and disquieted within yourself.

And you do give a rejoinder . . . yet only *internally.* What is this? All such things are but industrious engines of self love; these are proud secrets of your soul.

Self love which reigns in you stands as your greatest hindrance in obtaining precious peace.

22

Humility

There are two kinds of humility: one false and counterfeit, the other true.

False humility belongs to those who avoid esteems and who avoid all honor so that they may be taken as being humble. They go out of their way to speak often of just how very evil they are. (They do this so that they may be thought of as good.) Inside, they really do know their own misery yet they utterly despise the thought that *anyone else* would know. This is feigned humility; this is secret and hidden pride, nothing more.

There is also true humility. True humility never thinks of humility. Those who have it act with patience and live and die in God. They care not for themselves nor anything created. They suffer molestation with joy and desire nothing from it other than to walk in the footsteps of their despised Lord. They do not care to be thought of well by the world and are content with what God gives them. They are convicted of their own faults with *calm* shame!

There is no injury which can disturb them nor trouble that can vex them, no prosperity that can make them proud.

True humility is an inward thing and has nothing to do

with *external acts.* (Taking the lowest place, being quiet, dressing poorly, speaking submissively, humping the shoulders, shutting the eyes, sighing effectively, speaking of your own faults, and calling yourself miserable. Do you really think such conduct is going to convince *God* that you are humble?) Instead, there is *simply* knowledge: an understanding of what the self nature really is! It is an internal understanding, not carried about as profound knowledge. There is no sense of believing one is humble . . . not even if an angel were to reveal such things.

Two things must be discovered: the greatness of God and the vastness of the devastation of the fall as pertaining to your own soul. It is an understanding so vast that no tongue can express it. From this revelation proceeds a glimpse of the grace of God . . . a grace which takes pleasure in encompassing that person with the pure goodness of God.

****

You cannot be hurt by men. You cannot be hurt by devils. You can only be hurt by self, your own pride, and the violence of your desires. Your self is the greatest devil of all.

It is best that you have no desire to be esteemed. Remember that the incarnated God was called a fool, a drunkard, and one having a devil. And we are His followers! Yet we would desire to enjoy happiness and the approval of men. We would follow Him without knowing, without even desiring, an intimate understanding of His cross, the reproaches He knew, and the humility that was His!

True humility abides inwardly in the quiet of a man's heart. It abides there and rests there. If you think you have made any progress in this matter (especially if you think you have done it by being humble and by humbling yourself), then know you are not humble at all.

You have not even taken the first step in the way of living within the spirit. If you take refuge in excuses, if you exercise the art of replying, of defending, of attacking, then there is no humble heart within you. Replying to things said about you grows out of secret pride from whence self reigns. Excuse of self implies a lack of understanding of the true worthlessness of your self-nature.

23

Solitude

There are two kinds of solitude. There is an outward solitude when one simply does not speak, or speaks little.

There is also an inner solitude. Inner solitude means forgetting about everything around you, being detached from it, surrendering all purpose and desire and thought and will, and *then* coming before the Lord. This is true solitude. You will find it to be a sweet rest and an inward serenity . . . found in the arms of your Lord. For that believer who is able to stay in such a place before his Lord there will be a great number of discoveries.

For the believer who comes this far there is the discovery that the Lord converses and communicates with the believer in his inward parts. It is in *that* place the Lord fills the believer with Himself . . . but fills him only because that person is *empty;* He clothes him with light and with love because he is naked, lifts him up because he is lowly, and unites him with God and transforms him, because he is alone.

I see this solitude with God as a figure of eternal bliss — a picture of that future time when the eternal Father will be forever beheld.

****

With reason are you called solitude.
For you are so alone.
There is scarcely a soul that seeks you,
That loves and knows you.

Oh, Divine Lord, how is it that your
children do not go from earth to this
great glory?
How is it that they lose so great a good
Forfeiting it for things that are created?

Blessed soul, how happy you would be
If you would but leave all for God
Seek Him only
Desire nought but Him
Sigh for Him alone
Desire nothing —
Then nothing will trouble you.

****

If you desire any good, however spiritual it may be, let it be desired in such a manner that you be not disquieted if it is not granted you.

****

If you will simply, freely, give the Lord your soul, then step back, detached from all things, free and alone before Him, you will be the happiest person upon the earth.

If you would enter into this fellowship, then forget every care and every thought; put off self so that the love of God may live within your soul.

Dedicate your being wholly to your creator; offer your life in sacrifice to Him. (Do so with peace and quietness of spirit.)

The more the believer puts off his self life, the more he makes room for inner solitude with God. The more you become empty. both in outward things and in your own nature, the more room there is to be filled with the Divine Spirit.

Can you not see the Lord call you to enter into that place in your inner, central being . . . to that place where He will renew you and change you and fill you and clothe you and show you a new and heavenly kingdom?

24

Coming Before Him

The centermost part of your being, *there* is the *supreme region.* It is the sacred temple of the Spirit — the place where God delights to abide. It is there He manifests Himself to the one He created. He gives Himself in a way that transcends both senses and all human understanding.

It is in this place that the one true Spirit — who is God — dominates the soul and masters it, instilling into it His own enlightenment.

Do not misunderstand me; the highest place to which the soul can attain is a place of His will, a state of life composed more of the cross, patience, and suffering than it is of what men generally think of when they speak of *enjoyment.*

****

Please consider these things: How can you hear the inward and inspiring voice of your God when you also listen to the noise and tumults of others? How can you listen to the pure Spirit in the midst of considerations, of reasoning and logic?

That believer who has come to learn to dwell in this happy estate has two things to avoid. First, avoid that part of the self-nature that is in our human life. There is a part of you that is unwilling to die, but loves rather to be doing, and loves to be discoursing after its way. It is in love with its own actions.

Secondly, the soul must learn to avoid attachment to anything that is not the Lord. The mind, the emotions, and the will need to be set on God.

Further, as you come before the Lord there has to be a renunciation of all that is not God. You must come seeking no other interest upon this earth, neither some interest outside of you nor some personal interest within you. There is but one thing of interest with which you come before the Lord: *His Divine Will.* There must be within your prayer to God a pure, total, and absolute resignation of yourself to the hands of God — a *perfect* submission to His holy will. Come . . . busy yourself only to His pleasure. Come . . . interested only in His desire. Come . . . waiting with perfect submission, to receive whatever He has ordained.

Please realize that these things are only attained through an inward dying to an inward self, a death to inward inclinations and desires.

If the Lord does make progress in your life do not dwell on that fact nor allow it to enter into the secret thoughts of your heart. If you do, that thing will turn out to be a great hindrance to the Divine operation within you. Seek to remain as indifferent as possible to whatever the Lord does to you.

25

Things That are Spiritually Pleasurable

The Christian may ascend to a divine interchange of love with the Lord by two methods. The first method is by sensible pleasure. The second is by heavenly desire.

The first is frail. The believer is so frail that he must be stirred to Christ by outward drawings of pleasurable love. His relationship with the Lord has its foundation resting mostly on those things which bring pleasure to the believer. Remove those spiritual pleasures and the believer is on a very shaky foundation. But the kingdom of heaven suffers violence, and is not conquered by the fainthearted.

The second ascent belongs more to heavenly places. I will speak of three stages of ascent.

The *first* stage is that of the believer's being filled with God and obtaining *a hatred for worldly things.* In this stage the Christian is satisfied only with Divine love and learns to be quiet in the presence of God.

The *second* stage is *inebriation.* This is when the soul has more than it can hold. Within this stage there is born within the believer a fullness of Divine love.

The *third* stage is *security.* Here all fear is cast out of the believer's soul, and in that empty place which is left by fear's departure comes a Divine love. The believer resigns himself to whatever it is that Divine pleasure decrees. And when I speak of resignation to the will of God I mean the believer would be willing to go to hell if he but knew that this was the will of the Most High. There is a sense, in this stage, that it is impossible to be separated from the Beloved and from His infinite treasure.

26

Toward the Inward Way

There are five steps toward the inward way.

The first is *enlightenment.* In this stage Divine affection is kindled. Divine love for Him dries up those things which are but human.

There follows, secondly, an inward *anointing.* Something like a liquid Spirit flows into the believer's being, teaches him, strengthens him and allows him to receive deeper understanding of the Lord and His way. With this comes a pleasure that seems heavenly.

The third stage is *growth* of the inward man, the spiritual man. As the inward man begins to grow stronger than the outer man a clear fountain of pure love for the Lord arises.

Next comes *illumination.* Illumination is something coming from the Spirit of God to the human spirit which dwells within the man.

At last, there is *peace.* Tranquility. A victory over all fightings has come internally. Peace and joy are great. The believer seems to totally rest, as one abiding in Divine and loving arms.

By such do we ascend to the true Solomon.

27

Signs of the Inner Man

There are four signs by which you may know the inner man.

The first pertains to will and thought. The will is so trained that it engages in no act of love other than that which is toward God or pertaining to God and His purpose.

Secondly, when outward tasks are completed, the thoughts and will of the believer are quickly turned toward God.

Thirdly, if the believer enters into prayer, all other things are forgotten as if they had never been seen or known.

Fourthly, whereas the believer once feared the world, now he even fears the outward things of his own nature to the same degree he once feared the world. He shuns, therefore, not only the world, but outward things — except in those cases where charity requires outward performance.

Lastly, a believer who abides within the inmost portion of his being (within his spirit) lives in unbroken peace. Surely there may be outward combats, but the peace is not broken. There is an infinite distance between that inner place and the external tempest; the externals simply cannot reach this heavenly place. The believer can find himself even forsaken, opposed and desolate, but such a storm can only threaten and rage *without.* It has no power within.

28

Four Aspects of Internal Love

The secret and internal love which the believer has toward his Lord and which the Lord has toward him has four aspects to it.

The first is illumination, which is an experiential knowledge of the greatness of God and an experiential knowledge of the believer's nothingness.

The second is an inflamed love, a desire to be consumed with Divine fire.

The third is a peaceful and joyful rest.

The fourth is an inward filling of the Lord's power. The believer is replenished and filled with God. The believer no longer seeks, desires or wills anything except the greatness and the infinite good which is his God.

There are two results that arise from these four aspects of love.

The first is a great courage to suffer for God. The second is a hope — even an assurance — that the believer can never lose God nor be separated from Him regardless of outward evidence.

****

In this inmost place of the believer, Jesus Christ has His own paradise. It is to Him you ascend while yet remaining on earth and even carrying out the daily affairs of life. If you desire to really know who Jesus Christ is and if you look with singleness of heart toward your God, though you may be in adversity or desolation of spirit and in the midst of a lacking of anything and everything . . . nonetheless something within you stands firm and unshaken.

The constant and inner believer is one outwardly despoiled, yet wholly absorbed in God within.

****

Scientific information, rationale and logic are things acquired. You might say they are the knowledge of nature. On the contrary, the wisdom of God is something infused within us, and this infused wisdom brings us to a knowledge of the Lord Himself. The first — logic — desires to know what things should be attained and what should not be attained and how to avoid pain and effort. The second desire — an inner knowing of God and His ways — is characterized by not even wanting to know what it knows. Yet, there *is* a sense of deep understanding of so much. Scientific men — outward men — entertain themselves with the knowledge of things of this world. The truly wise live absorbed in God.

The man who has laid hold of a portion of Divine wisdom understands very clearly what his place in life is. He understands material things and even those things that belong to him. This is what makes this believer simple. He is not only enlightened, but balanced, whole . . . internally.

> But with wisdom there came to me all good
> things together.
>
> Proverbs 7:11

Most men live by their opinions and according to what they judge. They look about at things that are true and they look at the things that are false. A great many things come across their mind and imagination. They pay attention to the senses. But the man who has true wisdom judges by an internal truth which exists within him. It is the mark of a wise man to do much and say little.

The understanding of spiritual truth is actually hidden and shut off from most men, even those of theological learning. Why?

Because theirs is a scholastic knowledge. But there is also a *science* of the *saints.* This science is known only to those who heartily love and those who seek the end of their self-nature. The sermons and messages of men who have a great deal of learning and information, but who lack an experiential knowledge of the internal things of the spirit — such men can make up many stories, give elegant descriptions, acute discourses, elaborate theses . . . and yet regardless of how much it seems to be grounded in the Scripture, what these men give us does not contain the Word of God. It is but the words of men adulterated with false gold. Such men actually corrupt Christians, feeding them with wind and with vanity. As a result both the teacher and the one taught remain empty of their God.

Such teachers feed their hearers with the wind of sterility, giving stones instead of bread, leaves instead of fruit, and unsavory earth mixed with poisonous honey. These are men who hunt honor, making those things called *reputation* and *applause* idols to be sought after. They do not seek God's glory nor do they seek spiritual building within them. Those who preach with sincerity preach for their God. Those who preach without sincerity preach for themselves. Those who preach the Word of God while at the same time living in the spirit within their inmost parts, *these* men impress the Word of God upon the heart of the hearers. Those who do not, can carry what they say no further than the ear.

****

It is a maxim that will endure: To truly know the living God, *this* begets humility. To acquire learning, information, speculation, theory and theology and even Scripture, *this* begets pride.

You do not say someone is holy because he puts forth great ideas concerning the knowledge of God and the attributes of God.

Look for those who proclaim the love of God in great personal loss and self denial. You will find such wisdom far more among the simple and the humble than it is ever to be found among those who know so much about the things of God but so little of the Lord Himself.

****

How many there are who dwell in small villages, and who are so poor in human information, yet are so rich in the love of God. How many theologians and ministers we see immersed in vain wisdom, and yet so very poor in true light.

I would advise that you always speak as one who learns and not as one who knows. Nor should you be ashamed, but count it a great honor to be known as ignorant.

It is sad to say that even when men who are learned in Scriptural knowledge and in theology get some small spark of insight into the true depths of their God, it comes out of them as a mixture; it comes out not quite death and not quite Divine wisdom.

Unfortunately, this mixture of the natural and Divine is a great hindrance to pure, simple and true enlightenment of the wisdom of God.

29

Internal Discovery

There are two things which lead to a knowledge of God. One is far away and the other one is near. The first is speculation. The other is internal discovery.

Those who seek after a great deal of knowledge and information about the ways of God are really trying to satisfy their reasonings and to attain to God by means other than those of the *spirituals.* In no such manner can you attain a true and passionate love for the Lord. Such men who seek after God by the acquisition of information about God and acquiring information about the Scriptures are really nothing more than scholars. They do not know the unseen realms, nor do they realize that hidden things of God are found only within the spirit. Nor have they come to touch those joys which abide in the inmost depths of the believer . . . that place where God keeps His throne and communicates Himself to the one who comes and joins Him in that place.

Unbelievably, there are even some who condemn such a concept.

Why? Because they neither understand nor desire it. The theologian who does not find an internal way to his Lord misses that way because he is not seeking to enter by the gate which Paul speaks of when he says:

If any man thinks he is wise among you in this world, let him become a fool that he may become wise.

It has become a maxim among those who follow the internal way: *practice ought to be laid hold of before theory!*

This simply means that you should have some experiential exercise of having touched your Lord in a very real way before you start searching out knowledge and doing a great deal of inquiring about such matters.

The question, then, is: can learned men, theologians and mindy people, ever hope to learn such a path? Yes, *if* they will not rely upon themselves or set any value, they must rely upon their elaborate and extensive knowledge! Lay aside such things, forget them, and never pick them up in their pursuit. Rather, they should give their minds over to the simple and pure business of being in the presence of their Lord and beholding His face . . . without a great deal of thinking about what that should be, or how it is done, or images in their minds, or theories about what is supposed to come out of such a venture.

Any study, any seeking, any acquiring of information that is not for the purpose of getting to know the Lord is but a short road to hell. Not, I emphasize, because of the study, in itself. No, not at all. *But because of the wind of pride* which such pursuits beget. The greater part of the theological and learned men of our day are miserable because they only study to satisfy the insatiable curiosity of the human nature. Pagan philosophers do no more and no less.

Many such men seek God, but they do not find Him. Why? Because they are motivated more by curiosity than by a sincere, pure, and upright intention to be lost in God. They desire spiritual *comfort* rather than *God*

Himself. They seek Him not with truth, nor for truth, and therefore they find neither God nor spiritual pleasures.

He who does not seek his Lord with a will for self-abnegation will not find Him, nor receive the truth nor the light of the Spirit.

Rare are men who set a higher value upon hearing than on speaking.

Those men who have laid hold of the Divine wisdom that is within the place of the spirit are men who have been filled by their Lord with sweetness. He rules them with firmness and enlightens those who submit themselves to that light within. Where the Divine dwells, *there* is always simplicity and holy liberty. But craft and double mindedness, deceit, artifice, guile, and deference to worldly things are hell itself . . . at least to wise men they are!

30

Things to Abandon

The men or women who would attain to that deeper walk with their Lord must abandon and be detached from these four things:

1. Creatures
2. Temporal things
3. The very gifts of the Holy Spirit
4. Self

And lastly, they must be lost in God.

This last one (5) is the most complete of all. Only the believer who knows how to be detached attains to being lost in God.

God is more satisfied with the affection of the heart than with worldly science and thought. It is one in a thousand who sees the heart cleansed of all that imprisons it and pollutes it.

It is purity of heart which is the chief means of attaining to Divine wisdom.

****

You will never reach the ways I have discussed here if you are not steadfast — steadfast especially in those times when God purges you. He will purge you not only of attachments to temporal and natural goods, but of your desire for knowing His sublime blessing and things that have to do with unseen realms; for it is upon these very things that the self-nature sometimes supports and feeds itself.

****

Why is it that some people do all of the things that have been discussed here (and much more) and yet do not attain to an experiential knowledge of Divine encounter? It is because they do not subject and submit themselves wholly and entirely to God, who has light to give those who do. Nor do they deny, and allow to be conquered, their own self-nature. Nor do they give themselves totally to God with a perfect divesting of interest in themselves.

And finally, none of us as believers will be purified except in the fire of inward pain.

31

God or the World

All the basis for the loss of the self is founded in two principles. The *first* principle is to esteem yourself and things of the world very slightly. This means the renouncing of the self-nature, the forsaking of created things with holy resolution and energy.

The *second* principle is a great esteem for God. An esteem for Him that brings you to love Him, adore and follow Him without thought of personal interest even if that interest be very holy.

From these two principles will eventually arise conformity to the Divine will. This practical conformity to the Divine will — in all things — leads the believer to the death of the activities of the *self* and to a *will* that is in concert with God.

There must be no fixation on spiritual delights, nor even fixations on delights found in the unseen realms, and certainly not on emotions or affections. Such a road, if allowed, is filled with many illusions and disillusionments.

The proper path that you will take is one that includes the bearing of a very heavy cross. This road is the royal highway that leads to loss of self.

Can you understand that even honor and dignity and praise are matters that must be dealt with and put away? What place have these in your life? Would you compete with honor and praise that are for Him alone?

****

Why do so many believers hinder the Lord's deeper work within their lives? *It is because they wish to achieve something,* because they have a desire to be great. For this reason you find many believers attaching themselves to the gifts of the Spirit so that they may come out from that central portion of their being where they themselves are nothing; thus the whole work of the Lord in their lives is spoiled. They do not seek the Lord; therefore, they do not find Him. We find Him only where *He* is *all* and where we are nothing.

When one knows that he is nothing, then there is nothing that can disquiet him. He who knows he is nothing is incapable of receiving grievance or injury from anyone. Such a believer does not look on the faults of another, but only on his own; he frees himself from all his countless imperfections. As long as we can see ourselves as nothing, the Lord can continue to work in us, depositing His image and likeness within our inward being.

****

The believer who has entered into peace knows he is filled with God and with all those supernatural things which are a part of God. He is grounded in pure love, receiving equally those things which are pleasure and pain. He receives, in peace, whatsoever things come in the light or in the darkness, in the night or in the day, in affliction or in comfort. The believer lives in holy and heavenly indifference. That is, he never loses his peace in adversity nor his tranquility during tribulations, but is simply content in all things.

And should the very prince of darkness bring assault against that believer, he will not be greatly affected and he will stand firm. Both the high mountain and the deep valley are counted the same.

The valley of our outward being is filled with suffering, darkness, desolation. On the lofty mountain of our inmost being, the pure sun casts its beams, inflames us and enlightens us. The believer remains clear, peaceful, resplendent, serene.

This place of which I speak is the rich and hidden treasure. It is the lost pearl.

You are poor to look upon,
But inwardly you are full of wealth.
You seem low,
But you are exceedingly high.
You are that which makes men to live
A life divine here below.
Give to me, oh Lord and highest good,
Give to me a good portion
Of this heavenly happiness
And true peace
Which the world of the senses
Is neither capable of understanding
Nor receiving.

A Prayer

Oh, Divine Majesty, in whose presence the pillars of heaven do quake and tremble, You are more than infinite, and yet in your love the seraphim burn. Give me leave, oh Lord, to lament our blindness and ingratitude. We all live deceived, seeking this foolish world and forsaking You who are our God. We all forsake You, the fountain of living water, for the foul mire of the world.

Oh, children of men, how long shall we follow after vanity? What deception is it that causes us to forsake our Lord who is our greatest good? Who is it that speaks the highest truth to us and loves us most and defends us most? Where is there a more perfect friend or tender bridegroom or loving father?

Oh, Divine Lord, how few are those who are willing to suffer that they may follow Christ crucified, who embrace the cross. Oh, what a scarcity there is of those who are totally stripped, dead to themselves and alive to God and totally resigned to Your good pleasure.

The Life and Times of Michael Molinos

The Age of Michael Molinos

As I pick up my pen to write about Michael Molinos, I am aware that I am addressing the subject of one of the most controversial figures in church history. I feel, therefore, the need of creating some small historical setting as concerns the age in which he lived. Without such a context, an understanding of his life is not easily grasped.

The Roman Catholic church has a name for the people within it who are interested in a deeper walk with the Lord; they call these people *mystics,* a term almost totally foreign to a Protestant's ear. (I might add that only by the greatest stretch can the word *mystic* be said to be a Scriptural term.*) Molinos was a Catholic, and because he was devout and because he was interested in the deeper truths of the faith, he is referred to by historians as a *Catholic mystic.*

What is it this term is seeking to convey? It usually refers to someone who prays a great deal and who adheres to the traditional Roman Catholic teachings about the mysteries of God. But such a definition is an oversimplification.

*Don't be too critical; we Protestants have no word at all, Scriptural or unscriptural, to denote such people. Perhaps this is because we have had so few such people in our ranks that the need of a term has never arisen!

Mysticism has played a long, complicated, and very large role in the history and tradition of the Roman Catholic world. The Roman church has always made room within its walls for small groups of people who were passionately in love with Christ. (Do Protestants? Who knows! We will find out just as soon as we have our *first* such movement!)

It was during the 1500's that a kind of "deeper life" movement, a la Roman Catholicism, reached its all time high. The two most outstanding names of that era are John of the Cross and Theresa. Those two names will probably stand, forever, head and shoulders above all other mystics who have walked across the pages of Roman Catholic history.

Now, something quite interesting: Theresa and John of the Cross were both *Spaniards.* And why was it that the largest, and deepest, movement of this kind ever to sweep across Catholicism would originate in Spain?

To understand the answer we must look at the roots of Roman Catholic mysticism. In so doing we find Catholic mysticism to be founded as much on traditions as it is on Scripture! Like all Roman Catholic teachings, traditions and practices, its roots come as much from the Greek influence of Plato and Aristotle as they do from Scripture.

Take that statement as generally true; nonetheless, Spanish Catholic "mysticism" was less touched by this pagan and humanistic influence than was the Catholic mysticism found in other Roman Catholic nations of Europe. For example, take Germany. In the 1500's and 1600's the names Eckhart and Towler were the great Germanic influences of that day. Their teachings were — as is so typical of the German mentality — *rationalistic.* French mystics fell about halfway between the rationalistic bent of the Germans and the passion of the Spaniards. What "mysticism" there was in France during the 1500's was coming first from the influence of Richard and Heu of Saint Victor. (The general quality of what was coming out of France was far better than that coming from Germany.) But the Catholic mysticism of Spain had a far simpler touch than anything else in Europe, both in its teachings and practice. German mysticism was founded in conjecture, while that which was coming out of Spain amounted to a revival.

To illustrate, the writings of the Spanish mystics of that day contain far less reference to "the saints" and to the "Blessed Virgin" than anything found in Italy and Germany.

I hope I have not drawn too stable a picture of what is called *Catholic mysticism.* Every time there has been a *heart* revival among Catholics, there have been all sorts of controversies, claims, and counter-claims. In every case, from out of these controversies, there have grown up movements at odds with one another . . . schools of thought damning one another, and — always — a vocabulary! A vocabulary of terms and definitions which had meaning in that day and to that controversy. For those of us who live three centuries later all this thrust and parry, definition, terms, etc. can leave us baffled as we cast about trying to find a clear and simple understanding of what was really being taught and practiced. This is especially true for us Protestants as we wade into this wonder world called Catholicism of which we really know so little.

Quite frankly, Catholic mysticism really isn't all that fruitful a place for a seeker to go in quest of spiritual depth . . . but then neither is any place else that comes to mind.

To illustrate, one of the great "tests of fellowship" in the arena of Catholic mysticism during the 1500's was whether or not the person teaching his or her particular version was or was not following the doctrine of *antinomianism.* That's a big word which tells us some people taught that if the internal part of a person was drawn close to God, it did not matter what sins their body committed.

Another issue which Catholic mysticism fought over and one which a few occasionally drifted into was *pantheism,* or a close look-alike. Again, we have a big word which means "everything is God."

Generally speaking, Spain had been spared a great deal of bloodletting over all these issues during the period that spanned both the 1500's and early 1600's.

The Spaniards were a people of the heart more than they were of the head and spent less time conjecturing about what it was they believed and more time *experiencing* what they believed.

(This is not to exalt the believing community of Spain. There was another world of Roman Catholicism operating in Spain at the time — perhaps the most ruthless expression of violence the Roman Catholic church ever countenanced. Certainly it was the most militaristic. I speak, of course, of the Inquisition.)

To repeat, Catholic mysticism falls far, far short in revealing to us a way of laying hold of the heights and depths of the Christian walk as seen in the New Testament community of believers. Nonetheless, in the quiet monasteries and in a few small and forgotten places, most frequently to be found in Spain, pious priests and nuns and simple laymen were influenced by the writings of Theresa and John of the Cross — teachings a notch higher in quality than anything else being turned out in that day.

That brings me to the 1600's. It was almost inevitable that the leader of Catholic mysticism would be a Spaniard. The outstanding name emerging in the revival of Catholic mysticism of the 1600's was Michael Molinos.

Correction! The name Michael Molinos *almost* became the central figure of seventeenth century Catholic mysticism. Molinos' life, works, and teachings clearly reflect Theresa and John of the Cross. And in that simple fact lies a great deal of the explanation for both the success and the controversy Molinos was to engender.

You see, dear reader, Roman Catholic mysticism was but one of two ways to piety within the Roman tradition. Only *one.* There were very definitely *two* ways! Catholic mystics, practicing their way, made up only a *tiny* segment of Catholics in *any* generation.

The other way? Ah! Now *there* was a way to God and to piety that was far more popular than mysticism will ever be — far more adhered to, believed in, *and* practiced! Practiced, in fact, by virtually *everyone else!*

And what way was that? Piety, arrived at through *formalism!* And what is formalism, pray tell? It is putting our trust in outward observances, ceremony, ritual, traditions. (Do I hear a Protestant shifting nervously out there, somewhere?) From time to time, those two diametrically opposed influences have to clash. And one of the greatest clashes ever to occur in the history of the Roman Catholic church between these two very opposite views was during the 1600's. The three people most caught up in that clash were Michael Molinos of Spain, Fenelon of France, and Madame Guyon of France. Its resolution was not decided until, finally, it was settled by the Vatican itself! The outcome? Well, you can be sure history records that the organized church — be it Catholic or Protestant — has put to death far more people who were committed *to* the Lord than those who were neutral about Him.

I have always been taken with the insightful comment of Will Durant:

> The church has persecuted only two groups of people. Those who did not follow the teachings of Jesus and those who did!

Church history has yet to record an incident in which an informal faith — of the heart — ever won out over form and ritual within the walls of mainstream Christianity.

Still, I am a little awed as to how Michael Molinos managed to start the controversy that he did. He was a very orthodox Catholic, teaching orthodox *"Catholic mysticism."*

Of course, he did let slip one very minor yet quite unforgivable little blasphemy. In one small place he made a statement *that could be interpreted to mean* that it *might not* be necessary to observe the outward ordinances, rituals, and traditions of the church . . . and even hinting that confession and the taking of the sacraments were not necessary for one to know the Lord in a deep, meaningful way.

If you happen to be a non-Catholic, don't be too quick to "tut-tut." Broadcast that same basic theory among our Protestant circles and you may end up getting a reception not too dissimilar to the one Molinos eventually received.

There is a line, or type, of Christian wholly outside either Roman Catholicism or Protestantism, Christians who meet informally and who do not gather in church buildings, who have little or no formal structure. Until this day Protestants and Catholics alike look aghast at the oft-stated suggestion made by these odd believing believers that it is not really necessary to order your faith around the traditional Christian trappings of mass, Sunday morning church services, sermons, pulpits, buildings, etc., etc., in order for God to complete you in Christ. Be it Molinos, the Quakers, the Brethren, or whoever, that dares breathe such ideas . . . they manage to get in an awful lot of trouble. Those within the Roman Catholic church — and those within even the Protestant fold — who draw closest to the Lord seem, consistently, to lose interest in outward rituals, ceremonies, and traditions . . . and to get into hot water as a result.

Few, dear reader, have ever gotten in as much hot water as did Michael Molinos!

And so with this background presented, let us turn to the life of this man Michael Molinos, who was eventually to win for himself the title, "The Great Heretic."

The Life of Michael Molinos

The place was Saragossa, Spain. The year was 1627;* Michael de Molinos was born the son of a nobleman. It can be guessed that Michael was not the oldest child, as it was the tradition of the oldest child to take over the business and wealth of the father while the other sons became either lawyers, doctors, *or* — perhaps — priests!

As a student in the Jesuit College of St. Paul of Valence, Molinos was chosen to go to Rome to urge the Vatican to beatify a local Spanish Saint . . . Francoise Simon. You may choose as the date of his arrival in Rome 1669, 1670, or 1673. Like everything else about this man there is uncertainty and controversy. At that time he

*One source places his birth at Muniesa, Spain in 1640.

was not only a priest but held a doctorate in theology. He was author of a book entitled *The Brief Treatise on Daily Communion.* We therefore conclude he was already fairly well known as a man of piety.

The only physical description we have of Molinos is, "He was a man of medium height, fine presence, bright color, black hair, grave countenance."

Molinos had not been in Rome long before he attracted a great deal of attention, which seems to have grown out of both his personality and his teachings. Obviously he was not only a man deeply steeped in the Spanish Catholic mysticism of Theresa and John of the Cross, but also a man of some personal magnetism.

From what we can gather of the information left to us, he was a charming person, both in manner and in conversation, and brilliant in theology. Certainly he had a broad grasp of the entire scope of the teachings of historic Roman Catholic mysticism.

Many of the foremost families of Rome began to seek out Molinos as their confessor. He soon became one of the best known people in Rome.

One of the oddities of the story of his life is that he became the friend of many powerful churchmen, including Cardinals and, specifically, Benedict Odescalchi. If you do not recognize the name, perhaps you will recognize the title he later held: Pope Innocent XI. In the years to come it would be Molinos' friend Odescalchi who would be destined to preside over two of the greatest controversies — dealing with the deep things of God — that any Pope ever had to contend with. Specifically, the Molinos controversy and the Fenelon-Guyon controversy.

Molinos and Odescalchi were such close friends that it has been conjectured that Molinos and perhaps even Odescalchi carried within his heart the hope of reform in the practices of Roman Christendom.

The ascent of Molinos can be seen in the fact that he was offered living quarters in the Vatican itself. Never before — or since — has a man later to be officially declared to be a "heretic" ever lived that close to the apex of religious power.

Molinos rose to be the most trusted and esteemed confessor and perhaps the most influential clerical leader in all of Rome. As his popularity grew people flocked to hear him. Many made a commitment to his teachings and sat at his feet as his disciples.

From faraway France, Louis XIV sent a representative to Rome, one Cardinal d'Estrees, to check on this rising phenomenon; and even this gentleman was (at first) very approving of Molinos and his teaching . . . to the point of endorsing him and possibly . . . even following him. Nonetheless, dear reader, remember the name of d'Estrees and remember the fickleness of fame.

A monarch living in Rome at the time, Queen Christiana of Sweden, took Molinos as her Spiritual Director. (This act certainly did not take away any of his growing acclaim!) His sphere of influence grew until he was giving aid and advice to the great and near great of all Europe.

There was at this time what could perhaps be called a mini-revolt going on throughout European Catholicism against the formalism of the church. This revival-of-sorts was being expressed by something called Pietism in Germany. In Italy it would take on the much respected name of Quietism. In both Italy and Spain the Quietist movement was broadening its influence. Even in Protestant England there was Quakerism, the dissenting Protestant version of Quietism. In France it appears to have acquired no name at all, that is, until the term "Quietist" became a term virtually synonymous with heretic.

If you have ever studied history you have already

learned enough to anticipate what would eventually happen! Anytime something new within the world of religion gets popular it can only grow just so large and get just so popular before a reaction sets in; and woe betide those who stand in the way of that reaction.

That hour was remarkably late in arriving in the life of Molinos. He was after all a totally orthodox Catholic advocating that every person who sought a deeper walk with God also restrict himself to total obedience to his Spiritual Director. As to his teachings, Molinos was virtually "chapter and verse" Theresa and John of the Cross. He seemed almost not to be a teacher at all, but only an expounder of the teachings of Theresa.

Then who was there left to oppose this popular man? And on what possible grounds? In the early stages of his career in Rome his success was unbroken.

Molinos had become so popular and demands upon his time so great that pressure began to build for him to put his teachings into print. This pressure was greatest from a friend and fellow priest within the Franciscan Order named Giovanni de Santa Maria. And so, sometime in the early 1670's (1673?), Molinos sat down to write out his teaching, wholly unaware that he would author what was to eventually become the most hated, feared, damned, suppressed, denounced, and *burned* book ever to be penned by a Catholic.

The book was published in 1675 under the title *Spiritual Guide,* coming out about five years after Molinos had come to Rome. The book was nothing less than a smash hit. In the next six years, we are told, it was translated into every major language of Western Europe.

There appeared in the preface of this book something called an Approbation — a stamp of approval by well known scholars. In fact, this book was approved by no less than four Jesuits, all part of the Inquisition! It was pronounced to be "a priceless jewel of piety and perfection." (Keep that in mind. The *Inquisition* was to twice praise this book in lavish terms. Later it would issue a *Christendom-wide* ban on it.)

The Spiritual Guide was a clearly written book in contrast to the flowery style of literature of that day. It is doubtful that anything more clearly written on the subject of spirituality had ever appeared in the Italian language. It was shortly to make its appearance in four other European languages . . . a breath-taking feat even for our day. Very simply it became one of the most popular religious books of that age.

Just how popular and how influential was this book?

Cardinal d'Estrees, Louis XIV's representative, was the power behind having it translated into French. Cardinal Petrucci had a book based on *The Guide* written for nuns.

A growing number of priests were adopting Molinos' methods and were advising their people to follow the instructions within the book. Many nuns were laying aside their rosaries and other devotions to practice this *inward* prayer. Throughout Italy there were "unions" being formed by those who followed the teachings of Molinos.

In less than six years twenty editions of *The Guide* were published in Italian, Spanish, French, and Latin; the exact number of books this represents is not known. Molinos had become the spiritual leader of his age. Would he be stopped? Could he be stopped? Did he have adversaries?

Not yet. But when they finally arose they were formidable.

Molinos was saying that life itself was one continual act of faith and love to God. Such an idea stood in strong contrast to what other Jesuits had to say on this matter.

The Jesuits were great at asking philosophical questions and among them was the question, "How often, and when, are we obliged to love God?" The proposed answers were varied. Generally, the Jesuit would answer, "Our duty to God is every Sunday." "It is essential to love God at least once a year." "It is sufficient if, in an ordinary life, God is loved every five years." The Molinos idea was certainly far afield from this narrow concept.

Eventually the Jesuits would come to feel that they had found in Molinos' teachings the idea that confession was not necessary before communion. This would begin as a nervous impression, but their worst fears were confirmed when they eventually discovered that Molinos had not been to confession for several years!

But is this the heart of the issue? I doubt it.

What was the issue? It was fear. Fear of the emerging of a new power. Molinos was popular. He had followers. When "old" or established power sees new power emerging, it feels threatened. Unfortunately, the older power — the Jesuits — were themselves very powerful.

Wherein lay their power? In numbers! In land. In wealth. In influence. But most of all, in the throne of France.

Despite their unassailable power and prestige the Jesuits felt threatened by what they perceived as the competing influence of Molinos.

Dear reader, you can be sure that rarely — if ever — does the true problem within any Catholic or Protestant dispute emerge into the open. In all of church history's disputes, it is money, insecurity, someone else's success, power, spheres of influence, that are the underlying factors in virtually any Christian blow-up. Theology is but a convenient and effective smoke screen. All the foam and froth you see in public bears little relationship to the real, less obvious, more psychologically threatening issues.

Where did the first signs of opposition to Molinos appear? In the person of Father Paul Segneri, a barefooted priest — a kind of prophet — who dressed in rags and walked all over Italy denouncing sin. Segneri was a powerful and popular preacher. On this particular occasion he started across Italy preaching the necessity of repentance and proclaiming the greatness of the church to all who would listen. So powerful was his personality and so eloquent his preaching that when he began to approach a village the church bells would ring, and people would pour out of the town to strew flowers at his feet. (Obviously, we are not looking at our own age. It is doubtful any town in Christendom would do such a thing for any preacher today, be he barefooted or shod with horseshoes.) Leaders of the city would come out to greet him and lead him, in triumph, into the city. Obviously Segneri had a large and enthusiastic group of followers. So great, in fact, that guards had to protect him from his own popularity.

It was this man, Segneri, who first raised a serious challenge to Molinos. He had authored a collection of books and now published one entitled *Harmony Between Effort and Quiet in Prayer.* The age old battle line between faith and works, law and grace, realms seen and realms unseen, was being drawn. His book appeared in Florence in 1680, exactly five years after *The Spiritual Guide.* Father Segneri was careful not to accuse Molinos of heresy. In fact, he did not even refer to Molinos by name. He spoke highly of the inward life but insisted — in the best Roman Catholic tradition — that this was a type of experience and relationship to God that *only a few people could know.* (That is a vintage Catholic doctrine dating back to Thomas Aquinas and before). For ordinary people to follow these teachings was to expose them to great risks, he contended.

Does history ever vary?

Segneri gave Moses as an example of his point. Moses is one man out of a million people. Only one in a million is called to stand face to face before God.

Segneri also found something else he objected to, though he did so very gently. It is very difficult for those of us who are not familiar with Roman Catholic tradition to understand the point he was making. The Roman Catholics speak of two kinds of prayer. One is outward and one is more subjective. One is called "meditation" and the other is called "contemplation." Yet to a Protestant, to Scripture, the two words and the concepts behind them are utterly foreign. Molinos was saying, "Once you lay aside the first kind of prayer — meditation — you should never return to it but continue only in the second kind of prayer, contemplation." Segneri disagreed with this.

Segneri's book was not belligerent; it could not afford to be, as Molinos was simply too popular for a frontal assault. Nonetheless, here was the first evidence of an opposition which would eventually grow into a fire storm.

Segneri had really done a rather small thing. He had dared to oppose this enormously popular figure.

Just how popular Molinos was can be seen in that which happened to poor Segneri after he published his book. He lost his followers! He was treated as if he had been excommunicated. Threatening letters were sent to him; when he appeared in public he was received with scorn and derision.

But another attack on Molinos was soon to follow. It came in January of 1682. The Archbishop of Naples, whose name was Cardinal Caraccioli, wrote a letter to the Pope in which he recounted the "results" of what happens when people follow Molinos' teachings.

Here is a portion of that letter:

> Lately there has been introduced into Naples, and as I hear in other places also, a frequent use of passive prayer, which is called by some the prayer of pure faith or quiet. They usually refer to themselves as Quietists because they make use neither of meditation or vocal prayer, but when they pray, they remain as quiet and as silent as if they were either dumb or dead.

Caraccioli went on to complain that those who practiced this form of prayer *had given up their rosaries,* abandoned their *images* (including the *crucifix),* and had even given up the daily practice of *mass.* Furthermore, he reported, the number of people doing — or *not* doing — such things was growing daily. Shades of dissident Protestants, the man was reporting a revival!

(In 1685 a contemporary wrote — while visiting Italy — that there were 20,000 people in Naples following Molinos. He further commented, "The Jesuits have set themselves against it as it might weaken the empire of superstition and breed schism in the church.")

To hear news like this would be comparable to hearing that a group of churches in East Texas had given up Sunday Schools . . . that pastors had given up their titles and were getting jobs (*working* for a living?!) . . . that the Christians were meeting in homes and laymen were doing all the baptizing . . . and *nobody* was officiating at the Lord's Supper.

Now news like that might sound wonderful to some ears, while others might consider it the greatest horror of all the ages!

(Personally, I kind of like the idea!)

The Archbishop went on to ask if the Pope would please tell him how he should proceed against this new turn of events.

This letter placed in motion a grinding wheel that would crush — and eventually even annihilate — the work, the writings, the influence, and almost the very *memory* of Michael Molinos.

Perhaps we can pause here to draw some lesson from this experience.

Jesus Christ continued to be popular in Galilee and in Judea until that time when attendance at the Temple began to drop off. The religious leaders saw even the simplest people begin to change their traditional religious practices. That, by the way, is a rare historical event. (For instance, nothing has happened in 1500 years to change the way Catholics meet. Nothing in 400 years has altered even one iota the Protestant's Sunday morning ritual. Further, I suspect that a thousand years from now both will still be following essentially the same Sunday format that they do today. No, ritual virtually never changes . . . no matter how great the revival.)

It was doing this that crucified Him. Just a few years later the same thing happened in Jerusalem again. The second time it was the Apostles. And again, persecution set in.

Note, therefore, that a new movement can be tolerated until the religious hierarchy begins to lose membership and/or finances. When the most sacred traditional *ceremonies* and *practices* begin to be abandoned then the religious world *will* begin to persecute whatever thing it is that is causing the change.

Nor is such conduct confined to Catholics. Such is the way of any established segment of *any* religion.

Back to Molinos.

Enter the Jesuits.

Previously the Jesuits had backed Segneri's book. Now they backed the Archbishop's letters. At last, public opposition had broken out.

In the midst of all this the Inquisition intervened. They set up a commission in Rome to look into (to *inquire* into) the writings of Molinos and of Segneri.

The climate was changing rapidly. Men began that ancient struggle with *definitions.* Define a thing, then you can battle over it.

What was Molinos teaching? What was Quietism? Had this anything to do with the battle raging in France? Was this *free will* or *grace?*

Sides began to be drawn. Bishops, cardinals and scholars began to take sides. By 1681 the words "prayer," "meditation" and "contemplation" had become slogans of parties. Memoirs and epitomes were raining down upon the Holy Office.

In 1682, the commission assembled. They read the books in question, examined them carefully, and — would you believe — the book by Segneri was condemned! The book by Molinos was pronounced by the Inquisition to be *"in agreement with the faith of the church and with Christian morality"!* Segneri's attack was judged groundless and the people called Quietists had the approval of the tribunal. As a result Petrucci was made a Bishop, and the teachings of Molinos swept to greater heights of success.

This turn of events did *not* slow the Jesuits, but rather increased their search for an area of vulnerability. These men saw themselves facing something akin to German Protestantism and French Jansenism . . . in Italy! They saw this Italian revival of piety as potentially even more dangerous than Protestantism or Jansenism. This revival had the blessing of the Pope!

They saw their Pope wavering away from the Jesuits and toward Molinos. Failing, therefore, in the religious arena, they now turned to the political.

The Jesuits' greatest store of political power lay in France.

In France the teachings of Theresa, Saint John of the Cross and Molinos were really not all that widespread; therefore, the Jesuits had to find some way to instill their own fears into the heart of Louis XIV. How?

It was really easy. They tied Molinos to something *Louis* hated and feared.

At that time, there was a political-religious movement that was taking France by leaps and bounds. Called Jansenism, it was in diametrical opposition to the Jesuits. At that very moment a controversy was raging in France between Jansenism and the Jesuits. The French Jesuits were fighting tooth and claw to arrest the widening influence of Jansenism.

Over the years the most powerful monarch in Europe — and perhaps the most powerful monarch in all the history of Europe — had slowly moved into their camp. Fortunately for them Louis XIV was — religiously — almost entirely under the influence of a Jesuit whose name was Pere LaChaise . . . and of Bossuet (who was the Roman Catholic version of a Martin Luther). It was to Pere LaChaise the Italian Jesuits turned for help.

Now Louis XIV was a man easily aroused by the thought of heresy within the Catholic Church; convince him that something — anything — smacked of Protestantism and he was your instant ally. Louis had just gone to great ends to stamp out the Calvinists (the Huguenots) of France, and now he was having whispered in his ear that there was a heretical movement down in Italy so popular that it might fill the Huguenot vacuum.

So it came about that in the year 1685 the greatest monarch in Europe, and the most powerful man in Europe, presented his grievances to the Pope through Cardinal d'Estrees (Remember him? He was the French Cardinal who had earlier investigated Molinos and his teachings and given both his blessing.) Louis expressed his grief that favor had been shown a *heretic,* that there was being tolerated one who taught people to despise the order of the services of the church!

Do not think that power and money do not have their effect. Against what seemed to be deeply held religious convictions in favor of the Molinos revival, the Pope began to waver.

Once more, this dispute was turned over to a tribunal within the Inquisition. This *second* tribunal opened the floodgates of opposition.

In May of that year (1685), Molinos — along with his friend Petrucci — was summoned before the Inquisition.

Later, on July 18, papal guards were sent to his house and he was arrested. Michael Molinos was thrown unceremoniously into prison. In August Louis XIV wrote asking to henceforth be informed of all details.

As so frequently happened in those days, a friend of Molinos disappeared . . . never to be heard from again; such was the fate of the Jesuit Martin Esporsof. His crime? He embraced the practices of Molinos.

Next, Molinos' home was invaded. Twenty thousand letters were found! I am sure the Jesuits were horrified at what they discovered therein. Among these letters was correspondence with some of the most influential figures of Europe. Perhaps it was the growing realization of just how influential Molinos was, and the possibility there might come out of that influence a new unstoppable movement that the Inquisition and Jesuits could not control, that brought so great a fear into the hearts of his enemies. Whatever, there were 20,000 pieces of evidence that they could interpret any way they wished.

Every one of those 20,000 letters was burned. I am of the opinion that had they survived, despite all the attacks the name Molinos has undergone these 300 years, today he would be revered alongside Theresa and John of the Cross.

Why?

For two reasons. John of the Cross was a hated and controversial figure while he lived. Only the passing of time sainted him. Opposition, persecution and torture at the hands of one generation of Catholics has not deterred a later generation from bestowing sainthood on that person.

But I think even more the content of those letters, had they survived, would have vindicated him. As an author Molinos was a notch above his contemporaries. It is my opinion that the letters were destroyed because of their quality, *not* their heresy.

You must realize Molinos lived in a day before the telephone, the typewriter, and even before books had come into wide use. *Correspondence* literature was perhaps the most perfected and lucid of all literary art forms of that day. To put it another way, correspondence *was* an *art form.* There are many men and women of that age who are classified as literary "greats" solely on the basis of the letters they wrote.

It is my surmisal that going up in those flames was Molinos' rightful place in church history . . . and, for us, the loss of those 20,000 letters constituted the loss of one of the greatest spiritual treasures of all time.

In November of 1685 the Spanish Inquisition headquartered in Avagon, Spain officially condemned *The Spiritual Guide.*

It was all over for Michael Molinos!

Their Inquisitional decree reads as follows — certainly one of the strongest official statements ever made by a religious body:

> The writings are "judged heretical. We have condemned, noted, effaced as heretical, pernicious, erroneous, scandalous, blasphemous, offensive to pious ears, *all* writings of Miguel de Molinos. We have forbidden each and every one to speak of them, to believe, teach, keep and practice them."

For the next two years after Molinos' arrest, very little was heard of him or the controversy. Molinos had simply been swallowed up in oblivion. This was the wisest possible move his enemies could have made. Molinos' popularity began to subside; the people began to forget.

It was in the fading memory of Molinos that the Inquisition chose to make its final strike. Proceedings against him began in February, 1687. Unfortunately, dear reader, what took place has been covered in a cloud of obscurity for 300 years. Let it be said that, to this day, the Vatican has *never* published nor even allowed anyone to view the record of those proceedings or the subsequent trial. So obscured is the available information that it is not clear, even now, if there was a formal trial or only some kind of hearing. No one knows what took place inside those closed meetings. No one knows with what Molinos was charged nor what things were said about him; no one knows what wicked things were attempted against him.

I will tell what is known, and guess at what *probably* did take place.

First of all, the Inquisition made two very simple

observations within its confines: the teachings of Molinos, and others like him, had spread so widely in Europe that there was a possibility this move might become not only the primary force in Catholicism, but might eventually even arise to *control* the church. Secondly, they concluded, there were those who followed Molinos who rebelled against traditions of the church. That is, they disregarded the Mass and public worship, and (especially) they questioned confession and penance.

Having made these observations, the Inquisition was but one short step from concluding that Molinos was the instigator of a rebellion.

But you cannot convict a man that popular and get away with it without first making him a villain. Something had to turn public opinion against Molinos.

It is only here that we come to the reason Molinos holds such an obscure and controversial place in Catholic history. After all, he is a virtually forgotten man. And by those few who have not forgotten him there is a great reluctance to take his side or even to give him voice. Why? Why, with the passing of centuries, has this man been so shunned by history? The reason is formidable and I would be surprised, dear reader, if you have not already guessed the answer.

Rumors about Molinos — lies, if you please — were released in the streets of Rome. Most were ridiculous; but more tragically, those rumors have been left neither proven nor disproven for 300 years. Molinos waits, even to this day, for vindication.

And what were the rumors? First of all, his enemies gave his teachings a name, then damned that name. (It is a ploy as old as hate.) They called him an Alombrados.

The Alombrados were a sect in Spain that had once taught that prayers were worthless and that the only true prayers were ecstasy. This obscure group also taught that the sacraments were not necessary and that those who were truly close to God committed no sin. Unfortunately, an obscure accusation like that, tinted with the mysterious, and stated with scholarship, was easily believed among the masses.

Another rumor was launched and believed: Molinos was Jewish and had never actually been baptized. Anti-Semitism ran high in those days. The rumor had its effect.

Thirdly, his adversaries so twisted his teachings that they were able to say he was actually teaching subversion of moral conduct. This, they pointed out, was dangerous not only to the Catholic church but to the community.

Now, how did Molinos' enemies arrive at such a conclusion? His teachings subversive to morals? He taught, they said, that the unimportance of outward actions left a person free to do almost anything with his body just as long as he was disinterested in what it was he was doing. On this flimsy twist of his teachings Molinos was being crucified by the religious community.

It is possible the name Molinos would have survived in history if the rumors had stopped here. Unfortunately, they did not. The ultimate rumor was launched against Molinos, and it is *this* rumor alone which has destroyed Molinos' influence in church history, has caused historians to steer clear of him, and has left him and his writings without friend or defender.

Rumor is that at his trial (?) a number of women testified of having had sex with Molinos. This sex activity, his enemies insisted, was the ultimate end to which his teachings would lead anyone who followed them to their logical conclusion.

How many women made such public and formal accusations against him? One? Twenty? Two hundred? Or perhaps, *none?* No one knows. The rumors gave all sorts of numbers. And yet, with the passing of 300 years, even the rumors may have been only rumor. No one has the slightest idea if anyone spoke against him at his trial . . . on any subject. But those rumors, that such accusations were made, remain, even to this hour, to haunt and damn the name Michael Molinos.

Was he ever charged with immorality at the trial? Did the subject even come up? *No one* knows.

One historian observed that, of the facts actually known, his enemies only *theorized* that immorality would come of his teachings!

Who started these rumors? Did any of these rumors get dealt with at the trial? Or were they rumors so ridiculous that they never even made it to the courtroom? After 300 years we have no idea. All we know is that rumors were rife throughout Rome, Italy, and even Europe. If you knew nothing else of the man you would have heard that some priest down in Italy had seduced several hundred women. No man, especially a clergyman, could ever survive slander of that magnitude with his reputation intact.

Were such charges even remotely true? To even ask the question is to damn the man, because the very asking of it destroys him.

Because the text of the investigation and record of the trial have never been released the best anyone can do is guess. I will venture an opinion. I strongly doubt that Molinos' morals were ever even brought up during his trial. The virtue of his life was above dispute. Rumor was all they had against him, and only rumor could have suggested the idea of impure moral conduct. If there had been even the most remote truth to any of the tales, the *evidence* would have been broadcast from one end of Italy to the other. Had they been true the Vatican needed only to release the transcript of the trial. Instead the rumors were fanned harder, the proceedings clamped tighter. That those proceedings were *never* released thunders a weak — or non-existent — case against Molinos.

When, at last, charges were publicly released, *not one word of moral wrongdoing* on the part of Molinos was mentioned, or even alluded to. I think there is an excellent possibility that Molinos went through the trial, was sentenced, imprisoned, lived and died, never knowing that such a rumor even existed. The man is *innocent* until someone offers one shred of evidence that he is guilty.

By the time Molinos was brought up for judgement in 1687, the people in Rome were inflamed against him and clamoring for his death. Shades of Pontius Pilate. The story of his moral conduct had been told and repeated so many times that we would not be too wide of the mark to say that by the time of his public sentencing, some were seeing Molinos as not much more than a depraved sexual animal.

On February 9, 1687, two hundred of Molinos' followers were arrested, including priests! A number of people arrested were men and women of high influence. All were put into prison. The charge against them? They neglected going to mass, they neglected the ordinances of the church, or they had spoken in a way that slighted such things; they had taken communion without confession.

Next the Inquisition set up a commission to investigate the various convents and monasteries where Molinos' teachings had been practiced. The commission was geared to be shocked at whatever it found . . . even if it found nothing!

A new batch of rumors was spawned. Monks and nuns had given up saying the rosary, the crucifix had been abandoned, the only prayers being prayed were those inward, shapeless things. By now Rome was but one great rumor. More accurately it was a house of rumors.

Pressure was applied to the Pope. One rumor making its rounds stated that Petrucci had become a Cardinal because the Pope was a follower of Molinos. Another rumor stated that the Inquisition might even have the Pope examined . . . not as Pope, but as Benedict Odescalchi.

What of Molinos' trial? A better question is, was there a trial? It seems there was. Every word of it was taken down in Latin. The transcripts still exist. They have *never* been made public. Is it possible, now that Molinos has all but been forgotten by history, that someone with an eye for Latin and a mind like Sherlock Holmes will one day give us a straight answer concerning his life and his trial and unlock this mystery? I can think of no episode in church history that has so much evidence still in existence which cries out louder for revelation.

But we will not know *anything* until those records are made public by the Vatican!

You may wonder what Molinos gave as his defense. Interestingly, he refused to speak in his own defense.* Why? Once arrested he remained dumb. He sat there in silence, a testimony to his own teachings . . . "Take everything that enters your life with total acceptance and as from the hand of God." Blessing and persecution were to be counted the same and treated the same: as the will of God. It was his conviction about being indifferent to life's ups and downs that held him in silence.

*I am aware that at least one source said he talked, all through his trial; another, that he spoke not one word ever. I believe truth lies with the second.

You, as a reader, will have to judge whether or not this has been a good and spiritual way to approach the problems of life. If you ever choose to walk in such a way be sure it will not impress your enemies . . . nor win you acclaim. No one even seems to note such virtue. On the contrary, such conduct is an open invitation to be slandered. Adopt such a practice and be prepared to receive no better results than Molinos.

It appears that such a pious walk *escalates* hatred toward the one practicing it.

In the midst of all the scandalous rumors and electric excitement, a bombshell went off. The city of Rome was officially informed that Molinos had confessed he was a heretic . . . and that he had *recanted.* There was also released the ominous and damning statement that "he had also confessed other sins." To date, what those sins were has never been revealed. Further, Rome was now informed, the Inquisition had found Molinos guilty of heresy, and he had been officially sentenced to life imprisonment. Again, strong evidence there was no substance to the charges of immorality. Had they been true he would certainly have received the death penalty. This, as far as I can ascertain, was the first public knowledge that Molinos had been tried in court!

You can get some idea of how much the mind of the public had been re-programmed toward Molinos, and how much this life was still public topic number one, in this footnote: On the day Molinos recanted, every church in Rome rang its bells at the news. It was a day of jubilation for everyone.

What were the conditions of his recantation? Many felt he had been tortured. Others felt he was obeying his own belief that all men should submit to the church in whatever the church called for. There is no question about this: Molinos would have submitted to anything the church finally decreed, no matter what the conditions.

On the 28th day of August, 1687, an official decree was posted by the Inquisition declaring Molinos guilty of "having taught Godless doctrines and of having practiced them."

Included in this proclamation were 68 propositions stating that Molinos' teachings were "heretical, blasphemous, offensive to pious ears, insolent, and dangerous to the destruction of Christian morality," but never — to my knowledge — did they ever specify *anything.* All public statements ever released about Molinos were couched in vague generalities.

Not only did the Inquisition not give specific explanations, but it was clear it did not wish to do so. Was the Inquisition ashamed to let Christendom know the basis on which it drew its conclusions? One historian observed that everything which was publicly and officially said about Molinos was mild, and lacked enough weight to brand him a heretic or justify life imprisonment.

But on that fateful day of August 28, 1687, no one thought of such matters. Once the charges against Molinos were officially made public all copies of the *Spiritual Guide* — once officially acclaimed by the Inquisition — were ordered *burned.* Anyone found possessing *anything* by Molinos would be automatically excommunicated from the church.

Had Molinos really been on the verge of a great reformation movement within the Roman Catholic church? Had such a reform happened would the people of the Roman church, along with its clergy, have been brought into a deeper walk with their professed Lord? We will never know. The torch was so successfully put to this movement that 300 years later the question is unanswerable. The system had once again triumphed over liberty, the heart, and realms unseen.

What followed is one of those moments of history that is a caricature — almost a comedy — of justice.

The Inquisition set aside a day to make itself look good, look legitimate, and most of all, look powerful. It was decided that Molinos' renunciation of his heresy would be officially celebrated, with all the pomp of which the church was capable. (And it was capable of a great deal.) September 23 was set aside for this grand occasion.

Can you believe that the church issued a proclamation stating that any person attending this auspicious ceremony would be given 15 years of indulgences! With that a crowd of mammoth propositions was guaranteed!

The ceremony was held at a church called Santa Maria Sopraminerva. The recantation was to be made out in full view of the waiting multitude.

On the appointed day cardinals and bishops, members of the holy office, royalty (including princes), ambassadors and their ladies came . . . along with Rome's tens of thousands of ordinary people. So great was the throng that for a time the vaunted Swiss Guard seemed incapable of containing it. In the melee a number of persons were injured.

At some time during that day Molinos was given his last meal before imprisonment. The Vatican could afford to be gracious; we are told that it was a luxurious repast.

At some high moment of the celebration Molinos was dramatically led before the expectant mass. Molinos, 65, stood before them dignified and melancholy. Attired in the garment of the penitent, his shackled hands held a burning torch. He was conducted to a platform facing the cardinals and the tribunal. Around him were the ladies and the nobility, the priests, seminarians, and prelates. Someone mounted the pulpit and read aloud the charges against him; the reading took several hours. The crowd, we are told, became so incensed at hearing all that was charged against him that they began accompanying the reading with the cry, "To the flames! To the flames!"

Ah, we Christians do have a flair for persecuting one another!!

Following the reading came the pronouncement of judgement — Molinos was to be sentenced to life imprisonment. Within that lonely cell, the judgement continued, he was commanded to recite the Apostles' Creed, once daily; twice each day he was to recite the rosary; three times a week he was to fast. Confession was to be four times a year. As to the receiving of the sacraments, this was a decision left to his confessor.

After the reading of the judgement Molinos knelt down and formally renounced his heresy. He then signed a formal statement to the same effect, turned and received absolution from the commissary of the Pope.

At last, the thing was over.

(Mark that day as not only the end of Molinos' ministry, but the end of one of those rare revivals within Roman Catholicism — a revival which, had it continued even just a few years more, might well have changed the entire Catholic mind. With certainty it can be said that the Roman Catholic church passed up a rich opportunity to increase the spiritual depths of its priests and its people.)

As the ceremony ended, Molinos was led out of the church of Santa Maria Sopraminerva and, if records are accurate, escorted to a Dominican convent with the name of Saint Pietromontorio. A tiny cell within its confines would be Molinos' prison.

The door of the cell was opened and the prisoner was led to its entrance. Once Molinos walked through that door the world would forever be ridded of this troublesome Spaniard. Molinos knew that.

Well, dear reader, our friend Molinos also must have had a flair for the dramatic! As he walked to the cell he paused momentarily at its threshold. This was the last time his face would ever be seen. This was the last time history would hear his voice! The darkness of that dungeon was about to swallow him up into nothingness. Molinos paused, turned, and faced his adversaries. He fixed his eyes firmly on the Dominican priest who was about to forever seal that dungeon door.

What took place next is one of those rare and golden moments in history. An instant, a flash . . . an insight . . . into an otherwise almost unknown personality — a brief glimpse that tells volumes about a man, his character, and his inner being.

Here stood Molinos, one of those Christians of church history who have been attacked by other believers, yet who have chosen to remain silent while their life and ministry have been viciously destroyed. Now Molinos does the unexpected.

Far beyond any point when Molinos might save himself. . . far beyond the point when anyone could charge him with defending himself or with showing bitterness . . . Molinos broke his silence. At the last possible instant, Molinos *spoke!*

In fact, Molinos is remembered more for those last twenty seconds standing in front of that door than for all the rest of his life combined . . . and in this moment of revealing we see where this man's heart and mind really stood. Hear his exact words:

> Good-by, Father. We shall meet again on the day of judgement. Then it will be seen if the truth was on your side or mine.

What can we say? The man had been right and he knew it. His heart had not, could not, turn from truth which he knew lay on his side. He had submitted, yes. Outwardly. But inwardly he could not deny that which he knew and experienced of his Lord.

The door shut. The cell fell into darkness. The Dominican priest sealed the entrance. Molinos was never heard from again.

Now to finish this sad story.

In 1693, a rumor spread that Molinos had died. Like so many previous rumors this one proved to be false.

Four years later, in 1697, another Catholic priest — a French archbishop — had fallen under fire for his spiritual writings just as had Molinos in 1687. The most beloved priest in all France had been accused of heresy. The man? Fenelon!

Like Molinos in Italy, Fenelon had started a controversy in France so great that the issue would have to be settled by the Pope. As in Molinos' case a Papal committee was appointed to resolve the issue. Ironically, in the midst of the Fenelon dispute the church announced that Molinos had died — on December 29, 1697. He had been ill for three months, we are told. He had died, we are assured, in profound penance of his error and in full communion with the church.

(That was the official announcement.)

There were other reports that his illness had come on him mysteriously and had been due to poison. Like so much in this man's life, the truth will never be known.

What is left of Molinos today? Nothing except a small inscription on his tomb.

> Here lies the body of Dr. Molinos the great heretic.

That inscription declares that the Roman church looked on one of history's finest souls, a life lived in close relation to his God, and saw it as having no acceptable place within formalized religion.

I have read that there is, in a library in Munich, Germany, a manuscript entitled "Prosesso D. Molinos" which contains 263 propositions that the Inquisition put together as the principal charges of heresy against Molinos. It is my understanding that these propositions show clearly that the Inquisition dropped many of its original criminal charges against Molinos. Where were the charges of immorality? Where were the charges that he belonged to some heretical sect in Spain? Where were the charges of the immorality of his followers? They are not there. These 263 statements — unlike the investigation and trial, the proceedings of which were never made public — seem to bear very little relationship to the rumors that turned a city, a nation, and an international religious movement against him.

There is so little known that is certain.

We do know that Petrucci later stated in some writings that those things the Inquisition used to condemn Molinos were thoughtless misunderstandings of his true teachings, and that those misrepresentations were contrary to the truth.

You may wonder how Petrucci was able to make such a statement and get away with it. It was because, in the paradox of life, he had been made a cardinal, and one simply cannot treat a cardinal the way one can a common priest. Nonetheless, even as a cardinal Petrucci was summoned before the Inquisition privately, and eight of his writings were declared worthy of condemnation and were suppressed. Petrucci, faithful to that which he had been taught, submitted, and in his submission was allowed to return to his diocese.

After the imprisonment of Molinos, in both Italy and France, anything that even smacked of a teaching similar to that of Molinos was persecuted. Books were seized and burned. Literature of the Quietists almost disappeared from the face of the earth. Ritual, formalism, ceremony, and this wholly outward, objective relationship with Jesus Christ had once more triumphed.

Thrown out by the Catholics, unknown by the Protestants, we could almost say that the deeper Christian walk has been looking for a home ever since.

Certainly that deeper walk has never, since that day, made roots and spread its influence quite as deeply as during the latter part of the seventeenth century. The Protestant church, born in intellectualism and in doctrinal disputes, an affair almost entirely of the mind, has left little room within its walls for emphasis on a deeper walk with Jesus Christ. Catholicism reigned in its tolerance and gave such practice a far smaller place of influence than previously. Perhaps someday, in a very normal way (without excesses to the right or left), there will come forth among God's people a corporate body of people on this earth with pure intentions in this matter of the deep things of Christ. A people deeper in insight and experience than anything that has arisen during the 300 years which have passed since that dungeon door closed on the face of Michael Molinos and suffocated the strong voices of those who quested for Christ . . . in the depths.

904-598-3456 (fax) www.seedsowers.com

REVOLUTIONARY BOOKS ON CHURCH LIFE

The House Church Movement (*Begier, Richey, Vasiliades, Viola*) 9.95
How to Meet In Homes (*Edwards*) 10.95
An Open Letter to House Church Leaders (*Edwards*) 4.00
When the Church Was Led Only by Laymen (Edwards) 4.00
Beyond Radical (*Edwards*) 5.95
Rethinking Elders (*Edwards*) 9.95
Revolution, The Story of the Early Church (*Edwards*) 8.95
The Silas Diary (*Edwards*) 9.99
The Titus Diary (*Edwards*) 8.99
The Timothy Diary (*Edwards*) 9.99
The Priscilla Diary (*Edwards*) 9.99
Overlooked Christianity (*Edwards*) 14.95
Rethinking the Wineskin *(Viola)* 8.95
Who is Your Covering? *(Viola)* 6.95

AN INTRODUCTION TO THE DEEPER CHRISTIAN LIFE

Living by the Highest Life (*Edwards*) 8.99
The Secret to the Christian Life (*Edwards*) 8.99
The Inward Journey (*Edwards*) 8.99

CLASSICS ON THE DEEPER CHRISTIAN LIFE

Experiencing the Depths of Jesus Christ (*Guyon*) 8.95
Practicing His Presence (*Lawrence/Laubach*) 8.95
The Spiritual Guide (*Molinos*) 8.95
Song of the Bride (*Guyon*) 9.95
Union With God (*Guyon*) 8.95
The Seeking Heart (*Fenelon*) 9.95
Intimacy with Christ (*Guyon*) 10.95
Spiritual Torrents (*Guyon*) 10.95
The Ultimate Intention (*Fromke*) 10.00
Genesis *(Guyon)* 9.95
Exodus (*Guyon*) 9.95
Leviticus, Numbers & Deuteronomy (*Guyon*) 10.95
Job (*Guyon*) 9.95
Judges *(Guyon)* *9.95*
James, I John & Revelation (*Guyon*) 12.95

IN A CLASS BY THEMSELVES

The Divine Romance (*Edwards*) 8.99
The Story of My Life as told by Jesus Christ (Four gospels blended) 14.95
Acts in First Person 9.95

THE CHRONICLES OF THE DOOR *(Edwards)*

The Beginning 8.99
The Escape 8.99
The Birth 8.99
The Triumph 8.99
The Return 8.99

THE WORKS OF T. AUSTIN-SPARKS

The Centrality of Jesus Christ 19.95
The House of God 29.95
Ministry 29.95
Service 19.95
Spiritual Foundations 29.95
The Things of the Spirit 10.95
Prayer 14.95
The On-High Calling 10.95
Rivers of Living Water 8.95
The Power of His Resurrection 8.95

COMFORT AND HEALING

A Tale of Three Kings (*Edwards*) 8.99
The Prisoner in the Third Cell (*Edwards*) 5.99
Letters to a Devastated Christian (*Edwards*) 7.95
Healing for those who have been Crucified by Christians (*Edwards*) 8.95
Dear Lillian (*Edwards*) 5.95

OTHER BOOKS ON CHURCH LIFE

Climb the Highest Mountain (*Edwards*) 9.95
The Torch of the Testimony (*Kennedy*) 14.95
The Passing of the Torch (*Chen*) 9.95
Going to Church in the First Century (*Banks*) 5.95
When the Church was Young (*Loosley*) 8.95

CHRISTIAN LIVING

Final Steps in Christian Maturity (*Guyon*) 12.95
Turkeys and Eagles (*Lord*) 8.95
Life's Ultimate Privilege (*Fromke*) 10.00
All and Only (*Kilpatrick*) 7.95
Adoration (*Kilpatrick*) 8.95
Bone of His Bone (*Huegel*) 8.95

Call for a free catalog at 800.228.2665